Student Stress:
Effects and Solutions

by Neal A. Whitman, David C. Spendlove, and Claire H. Clark

ASHE-ERIC Higher Education Research Report No. 2, 1984

Prepared by

 ® *Clearinghouse on Higher Education*
The George Washington University

Published by

Association for the Study of Higher Education

Jonathan D. Fife,
Series Editor

Cite as:
Whitman, Neal A.; Spendlove, David C.; and Clark, Claire H.
Student Stress: Effects and Solutions. ASHE-ERIC Higher
Education Research Report No. 2. Washington, D.C.: Associa-
tion for the Study of Higher Education, 1984.

The ERIC Clearinghouse on Higher Education invites individuals
to submit proposals for writing monographs for the Higher
Education Research Report series. Proposals must include:
1. A detailed manuscript proposal of not more than five pages.
2. A 75-word summary to be used by several review committees
   for the initial screening and rating of each proposal.
3. A vita.
4. A writing sample.

ISSN 0737-1292
ISBN 0-913317-11-X

ERIC° **Clearinghouse on Higher Education**
The George Washington University
One Dupont Circle, Suite 630
Washington, D.C. 20036

ASHE **Association for the Study of Higher Education**
One Dupont Circle, Suite 630
Washington, D.C. 20036

This publication was partially prepared with funding from the
National Institute of Education, U.S. Department of Education,
under contract no. 400-82-0011. The opinions expressed in this
report do not necessarily reflect the positions or policies of NIE
or the Department.

Richard Lonsdale
Professor of Educational Administration
New York University

Linda Kock Lorimer
Associate General Counsel
Yale University

Virginia B. Nordby
Director
Affirmative Action Programs
University of Michigan

Eugene Oliver
Director, University Office of School & College Relations
University of Illinois–Champaign

Harold Orlans
Lawyer

Marianne Phelps
Assistant Provost for Affirmative Action
The George Washington University

Gary K. Probst
Professor of Reading
Prince Georges Community College

Robert A. Scott
Director of Academic Affairs
State of Indiana Commission for Higher Education

Cliff Sjogren
Director of Admissions
University of Michigan

Al Smith
Assistant Director of the Institute of Higher Education &
   Professor of Instructional Leadership & Support
University of Florida

CONTENTS

FOREWORD

A faculty/administrator discussion of student stress generally generates a variety of emotional responses. From the hardliners or academic elitists, the response is one of indifference that can be summed up with President Harry Truman's: "If you can't stand the heat, get out of the kitchen." The opposite reaction, often held by counselors and student personnel workers, focuses on a desire to minimize or eliminate all stress faced by students due to the belief that it has a negative effect on learning.

Authors Neal A. Whitman, Director of Educational Development in the Department of Family and Community Medicine, David C. Spendlove and Claire H. Clarke, both faculty members in the School of Medicine, all of the University of Utah, demonstrate in this report that stress can be both positive and negative. It can help achieve an institution's goals, but also can be a destructive force with very negative consequences. Therefore, it is extremely important for faculty members and administrators to be well aware of the results of student stress when they evaluate and develop academic and administrative policies and procedures.

With an understanding of the research on stress and coping, faculty members and administrators can better:

- evaluate the student's environmental setting,
- identify the sources of stress,
- make informed judgements on changes needed in order not to exceed the "optimal level" of stress—that **delicate balance of the positive and negative factors.**

By so doing, faculty and administrators can provide an educational atmosphere with maximum learning and social growth that avoids the extreme levels of stress that contribute to unnecessarily high student attrition rates.

Jonathan D. Fife
Series Editor
Professor and Director
ERIC Clearinghouse on Higher Education
The George Washington University

EXECUTIVE SUMMARY

What Is Stress and How Does It Affect Students?
Stress is any situation that evokes negative thoughts and feelings in a person. The same situation is not evocative or stressful for all people, and all people do not experience the same negative thoughts and feelings when stressed. One model that is useful in understanding stress among students is the person-environment model. According to one variation of this model, stressful events can be appraised by an individual as "challenging" or "threatening" (Lazarus 1966). When students appraise their education as a challenge, stress can bring them a sense of competence and an increased capacity to learn. When education is seen as a threat, however, stress can elicit feelings of helplessness and a foreboding sense of loss.

A critical issue concerning stress among students is its effect on learning. The Yerkes-Dodson law (1908) postulates that individuals under low and high stress learn the least and that those under moderate stress learn the most. A field study (Silver 1968) and laboratory tests (Hockey 1979) support the notion that excessive stress is harmful to students' performance.

Mechanisms that explain why students perform badly under stress include "hypervigilance" (excessive alertness to a stressful situation resulting in panic—for example, overstudying for an exam) and "premature closure" (quickly choosing a solution to end a stressful situation—for example, rushing through an exam).

Stressful events can be appraised by an individual as "challenging" or "threatening."

What Is Stressful for Undergraduates?
Students react to college in a variety of ways. For some students, college is stressful because it is an abrupt change from high school. For others, separation from home is a source of stress. Although some stress is necessary for personal growth to occur, the amount of stress can overwhelm a student's ability to cope.

Since World War II, changes in American higher education include growth in the size and complexity of institutions and increased diversity among students. A consequence of that rapid growth has been a loss of personal attention to students. One measure of excessive stress, that is, *distress,* in college students is the use of mental health services. Although some students may bring psychiatric problems to the college campus, symptoms commonly reported by campus psychiatrists portray a general picture of school-related stress, for example, the inability to do school work and the fear of academic failure (Ellis 1969).

A second measure of distress in college students is the dropout rate. Although nationwide figures are difficult to obtain, it is estimated that 50 percent of entering freshmen do not finish college four years later (Hirsch and Keniston 1970). Studies of college dropouts associate dropping out with the aversive side of the "fight or flight" formula; that is, students, feeling a mismatch between themselves and their college, wish to distance themselves from the source of stress, the college environment (Falk 1975; Hirsch and Keniston 1970; Katz et al. 1969).

Solutions suggested for reducing distress in college students include "stress inoculation"—for example, informing students in advance of what difficulties they might face and encouraging them to develop their own strategies to achieve personal goals. Other suggestions include improving campus mental health services and organizing peer counseling and self-help groups.

What Is Stressful for Graduate Students?
The accelerated growth in undergraduate programs has also been felt in graduate schools, resulting in an oversupply of Ph.D.s. Consequently, graduate students, facing poor employment opportunities when they finish their doctoral programs, feel stress associated with the uncertainty of their career choice and future prospects.

Often, graduate students perceive that faculty exert great power over their lives and feel that they live in a state of substantial powerlessness (Altbach 1970). Another source of stress is the difficulty of achieving social intimacy. Either it is difficult to find a mate or maintain a relationship with an existing one. Graduate students tend to lack the time, the opportunity, or both to develop interpersonal relationships (Hartshorn 1976).

Specific tasks that produce stress in graduate students are preliminary exams and the doctoral dissertation. Fear of academic failure related to these tasks is a definite stressor (Kjerulff and Wiggins 1976; Kolko 1980).

Solutions for alleviating distress include improved orientation for new graduate students, more flexibility in core requirements, and expanding the role of faculty advisors.

What Is Stressful for Law Students?

The Socratic method, developed at Harvard in the 1870s, still characterizes law education today. Certain problems are associated with the approach, however. It puts the teacher in complete control of the classroom, leaving students with little control over how they relate to the material being taught in class. Related to the Socratic method is the issue of feedback. Law students receive little feedback in class and little feedback about their academic performance until after first semester exams (Ellinwood, Mayerson, and Paul 1983).

Law students feel that grades are emphasized excessively and see the law school as a screening program for law firms, the best of which interview only students who have made law review. Often, when students do not rank near the top of their class at the end of the first semester, they give up trying because their best efforts were not rewarded (Silver 1968).

In an effort to deal with the lack of feedback, some students rely on bogus feedback; for example, students who do well in an ungraded legal writing seminar believe they will rank high in the class. The extent to which students rely upon false feedback to relieve their anxieties might be counterproductive if they begin to avoid adequate preparation for exams.

Suggestions to relieve distress among law students include giving earlier and more frequent exams, providing positive feedback in class, deemphasizing grades, and basing appointment to the law review on writing skills rather than on class rank (Ellinwood, Mayerson, and Paul 1983).

What Is Stressful for Medical Students and Residents?

Medical education includes four years of medical school and three to five years of residency training in a teaching hospital. Premedical education in college is in itself stressful because of the keen competition to get into medical school. Competition continues in medical school among students eager to get into the residency program of their choice. For some residents, competition continues for those who wish to earn the status of "chief resident" in the program and to win a postresidency fellowship.

A major stressor for first-year medical students is the amount and complexity of material to be learned. Students feel academic pressure because nearly all their classmates were superior college students (Gaensbauer and Mizner 1980). Fatigue is often cited as a stressor in the second year, and many researchers describe a hypochondriacal phenomenon by which medical students imagine they have the disease they are studying (Bojar 1971; Saslow 1956).

In the third year, medical students begin patient care, but they are low on the totem pole. Acceptance of death and dying emerges as a key issue in coping with stress. For some medical students, the clinical years become routine and the fourth year is less stressful.

When medical school graduates enter the first year of residency training (the internship), they find themselves again low on the totem pole, and overwork and sleep deprivation become major stressors. Lack of personal time continues to stress residents in their second and third years.

Solutions to help medical students and residents cope with stress include improving orientation for first-year medical students and residents. Better counseling and more support groups are recommended. Providing more free time in the medical school curriculum and residency training is often cited, but the requirements to achieve competency in medicine seem to preclude major reductions in the workload.

What Overall Approaches Are Recommended?

Stress is necessary to challenge students to learn. What is needed are approaches to reduce the negative aspects of stress (distress) that lessen students' learning and perform-ance. The key to reducing distress is providing students with a feeling of control over their education, information about what to expect, and feedback regarding what can be done to improve their performance. Students who do not feel helpless will adopt their own coping strategies.

Reactive coping, that is, dealing with one's own thoughts and feelings, can be facilitated by accessible professional and peer counseling, student support groups, and adequate faculty advising. Active coping, that is, dealing with the actual stressful situations or events, can be strengthened by providing students with early success.

Good teaching can not be overestimated as a key to preventing and minimizing distress among students. Of course, faculty may not be good teachers if they are themselves stressed and if they feel unrewarded for good teaching. How to reduce stress among faculty and reward good teaching are questions for further study.

It is Monday morning, and when I walk into the central building I can feel my stomach clench. For the next 5 days I will assume that I am somewhat less intelligent than anyone around me. At most moments, I'll also suspect that the privilege I enjoy was conferred as some kind of peculiar hoax. I will be certain that no matter what I do, I will not do it well enough; and when I fail I know that I will burn with shame. By Friday my nerves will be so brittle from sleeplessness and pressure and intellectual fatigue that I will not be certain I can make it through the day. After years off, I have begun to smoke cigarettes again; lately, I seem to be drinking a little every night. I do not have the time to read a novel or magazine and I am so far removed from the news of the world events that I often feel as if I've fallen off the dark side of a planet. I am distracted at most times and have difficulty keeping up a conversation, even with my wife. At random instances, I am likely to be stricken with acute feelings of panic, depression, indefinite need, and the pep talks and irony I practice on myself only seems to make it worse (Turow 1977, p. 9).

These thoughts, feelings, and behaviors of a first-year law student describe many of the symptoms associated with stress and some insight into how one can cope with feelings of powerlessness in a stressful situation. This chapter examines concepts of stress and coping and how these concepts relate to being a student. First, it discusses how stress and coping are related. Second, it describes stress, paying particular attention to problems with its definition and the models that are used to help understand it. Third, it describes coping, also discussing problems with its definition and the different ways people cope. Finally, the chapter discusses how stress and coping relate to the role of student and how colleges and universities can help reduce destructive forms of stress.

The Relationship between Stress and Coping
The concepts of stress and coping are neutral. Although people commonly see stress as negative and coping as positive, the relationship is not that simple. Stress can be psychologically positive or negative, and the means of coping can be effective or ineffective in meeting the chal-

lenge presented by the stressful situation. The potential for stress to be either positive or negative was described nearly 80 years ago: Individuals under no stress or extreme stress learn the least and those under optimum levels of stress learn the most (Yerkes and Dodson 1908). In other words, a curvilinear relationship in the form of an inverted U exists between stress and learning. A more recent look at this relationship cites several supporting studies of animals and humans (Hockey 1979).

This same curve can be used to describe coping. McClelland et al. (1953) used a ring-toss game with school children that demonstrated how the Yerkes-Dodson law works. They found that some children coped with the challenge of tossing the ring onto a post by standing directly over the post so that they were always successful. A second group of children stood so far away from the post that it was almost impossible to achieve success. While it appeared that the second group were creating the greatest challenge for themselves, both groups were actually comprised of children who were "low-need achievers." The second group, seemingly greatly challenged, were actually left with a convenient excuse. By making the task too difficult, they were not responsible for failure. A third group was described as "high-need achievers." These children dealt with the challenge in the game by making the toss difficult but achievable. The high-need achievers continually adjusted their position to the post so that they were continually challenged but not overwhelmed.

This phenomenon can be likened to the "overload principle" in biology (Hershey and Blanchard 1972); for example, in weight lifting, one can increase strength by lifting weights that are difficult but realistic enough to stretch muscles. Strength cannot be increased by performing tasks that are too easy or that will injure muscles. Likewise, effective coping requires recognizing the extent of the stress one is experiencing and balancing resources to avoid overcompensation or undercompensation.

Balancing resources for coping is similar to the biological notion of homeostasis, a concept developed by the physiologist Bernard in the late nineteenth century (Selye 1976). One of the most characteristic features of living beings is the ability to maintain the constancy of their internal environment despite changes in the surroundings. This power

Individuals under no stress or extreme stress learn the least and those under optimum . . . stress learn the most.

to maintain constancy later became known as homeostasis. A simple metaphor helps illustrate this concept. When windows are opened to the cold air, an added stress is introduced so that the furnace makes every effort to maintain room temperature. More fuel for the furnace is required to maintain constancy. Similarly, when students are taxed with a psychological stressor, increasing amounts of energy are required to keep them psychologically balanced. When coping with the stress of a difficult exam, for example, students maintain psychological balance by temporarily cutting back on socializing, spending more time studying, and planning to take a day off from studies after the exam.

What Is Stress?
Defining and describing stress poses major conceptual problems. Reactions to stress have been described as arousal, depression, anxiety, boredom, anger, physical discomfort, and discomfort in general. The physical symptoms associated with psychological and physical stress are changes in heart rate, blood pressure, and skin conductancy and various hormonal responses. In addition to physical symptoms, stressful situations produce psychological, cognitive, behavioral, and social reactions. A classic study of stress among graduate students defines stress as "discomforting responses of persons in particular situations" (Mechanic 1978, p. 7). This definition deemphasizes stress in terms of the nature of the event and emphasizes it according to the meaning individuals give to it.

Although this definition helps clarify an unwieldy concept, it also suggests some important questions about stress. Is stress a situational or a behavioral response? For example, when a student is faced with an exam, is stress produced by the exam itself or the way the student responds to the exam? If stress is the response, how is it different from coping? For example, is worrying about a test an example of stress or of coping? How many people have to act in a distressed manner for a situation to be considered stressful? And finally, how intense must the reaction to the stressful situation be to be considered stressful?

Despite the vast amount of research on stress, an understanding of the concept is still limited and plagued with problems (Chan 1977; Payne, Todd, and Burke 1982). In fact, not until 1966 was a distinction made between challenging and threatening stressors (Lazarus 1966). Positive stress is associated with situations that provide challenge and growth, but negative stress—or distress—is associated with threatening situations. One problem with the research is that it has not been adequately designed to look at causal relationships (Payne, Todd, and Burke 1982). Another problem is that too many studies focus on determining personality traits related to stress and coping. Yet personality traits have not been successful predictors of how people cope and thus who is at risk for distress (Folkman 1982).

Much of the literature on stress takes a fairly static view of the concept (Folkman 1982). What makes the phenomenon of stress so complex, however, is that it is dynamic, partly because as individuals cope with stress, they learn to adapt; thus, what is stressful is constantly changing. Mechanic's definition (1978), which reflects the inherent individual nature of stress, allows for this dynamic quality; it is perhaps the most adequate definition of the concept to date.

Brief definitions, however, do not sufficiently describe concepts. Various stress *models* are necessary to more fully understand the concept.

Models
Three stress models—the medical-biological, the psychoanalytical, and the person-environment—are discussed in the literature. Hans Selye, a physician, is probably identified with the medical model more than any other individual. Selye's model includes both psychological and biological stressors and is more commonly known as the general adaptation syndrome (Selye 1982). This model describes the way in which the body's biochemical defenses mobilize in response to psychological and biological demands (Selye 1982). The biological way in which humans adapt to environmental demands is similar to biological responses of other animals and even plants.

The general adaptation syndrome is a three-stage biological process in response to a stressor. In the initial stage, called the alarm reaction, the body makes a biochemical response in an effort to mobilize defensive forces. During the alarm reaction, the body becomes overwhelmed and dies or enters a second stage, called resistance, in which it responds in a different biochemical way. If the body is unable to adjust because of the severity and continued exposure to stress, the third stage, exhaustion, results. The body's ability to adapt is finite, and with continued exposure it gradually wears out, similar to a machine. Although Selye's model (sometimes called the "wear and tear" model) has been used to explain psychological stress, other research shows that the body reacts very differently to stress, depending on whether the stressor is biological or psychological (Baum, Singer, and Baum 1981).

The psychoanalytical model focuses on the individual's conflicts between biological and societal pressures. Freud referred to defenses as efforts made to protect oneself from instinctual biological demands that are in conflict with environmental pressures (Mechanic 1978). Freud's daughter, Anna Freud, later specified nine possible defense mechanisms the ego uses when the individual is anxious—regression, repression, reaction formation, isolation, undoing, projection, introjection, turning against the self, and reversal. These defense mechanisms have in common the characteristics of denial, falsification, and the distortion of reality, and they operate at an unconscious level. Although Mechanic mentions a few studies in which the psychoanalytical framework has been used to study stress, this model suffers from a lack of validity, particularly in relation to students. Because psychoanalysis was developed to understand neurotic behaviors rather than normal reactions to stress, the model does not take into account healthy aspects of effective problem solving in which denial, falsification, and distortions of reality are not necessarily used. The model is not used to look at factors that contribute to stress in the environment; rather, it focuses on intrapsychic processes.

The person-environment model appears to be most appropriate for understanding stress among students. Although the model has a number of variations, its basic components include "the external and internal forces of stimulus conditions of stress reactions and the intervening structures and processes that determine when and in what form the stress reactions will occur" (Lazarus 1966, p. 13).

What makes an event stressful is the degree to which it is perceived as threatening, harmful, or challenging (Lazarus 1966). When an event is appraised as challenging, overcoming the stressor seems more hopeful, but when it is appraised as threatening, a sense of potential loss and the need to avoid the stressor are apparent. The distinction between challenge and threat is important because individuals who are inclined to see events as challenging demonstrate more confidence in their ability to adapt and will cope differently from those who picture the same event as threatening (Baum, Singer, and Baum 1981). Appraising a situation as threatening can evoke a response that is even more harmful than the actual event; therefore, secondary appraisals are used to weigh the dangers and benefits associated with the initial response (Lazarus 1966). Thus, individuals are continually involved in a dynamic process of appraisal and reappraisal of the stressful situation and their reactions to it. Because each individual responds to the environment differently, this view constitutes a person-environment model of stress.

A crucial aspect of the appraisal is control. Numerous studies support the idea that having control and perceiving oneself as having control over adverse outcomes have the effect of reducing stress: "If I can stop the roller coaster, I don't want to get off" (Miller 1980). Predicting and receiving information about adverse outcomes also help one feel in control and appear to be as beneficial as actually having control (Glass and Singer 1972). These concepts work together in this way:

> *Someone in the neighborhood is throwing a big, noisy party. Neighbor A is told to complain if he can no longer tolerate the music and frivolity, although he refrains from doing so because of self-imposed restraint, etc. Neighbor B receives no such communication. The party festivities are equally disruptive to the neighbors. Despite this it is likely that Neighbor A (who believes that he can complain but never does) will be less disrupted by the festivities than will Neighbor B (who will probably spend the whole night stewing and might eventually tip off the police as a "concerned citizen")* (Miller 1980, p. 71).

Neighbor A experienced less stress because he received information about controlling the situation. The fact that he chose not to exert control made no difference because he at least had the perception of being in control. Neighbor B was more disturbed because nothing suggested he had control. Furthermore, Neighbor B will experience increasing levels of stress if he sees himself as helpless (Abramson, Garber, and Seligman 1980).

Three basic sources of situational stress represent the environmental side of the person-environment model (Lazarus and Cohen 1977). First are cataclysmic events—sudden and powerful events affecting large numbers of people, such as war, natural disasters, or economic depression. The second source of stress is similar in its suddenness and powerfulness, but it differs in that few people are affected. Such events include illness, death, personal failure, or any personal loss. It is important to distinguish between these two sources of stress because it is likely that less psychological damage occurs during cataclysmic events where more people can share their emotions and compare their behavior with others. The third category of stress involves "daily hassles"—ongoing and chronic problems for which one has adapted at some level but that still can take a psychological toll over time. Such problems include dissatisfaction with one's marital relationship, living in a crowded environment, and problems with traffic to and from work.

The person-environment model is a general and simple explanation of psychological stress that is widely accepted in the literature. The model provides a useful framework for analyzing psychological stress experienced by students. The educational environment combined with students' thoughts and psychosocial backgrounds form the essential ingredients necessary to understand stress among students.

Coping

Stress and coping work together in a balance. "Coping behaviors seem to be directly related to characteristics of the source of stress" (Baum, Singer, and Baum 1981, p. 24). Characteristics of the source of stress change at least in the mind of the individual, depending upon the coping mechanism used.

A major reason for confusion about coping is that no
adequate theoretical framework or classification system
exists for understanding the concept (Folkman 1982). Research on coping is oriented too much toward personality
traits, an approach that assumes individual behavior is similar in different situations (Folkman 1982). But coping is a dynamic process that occurs within the person-environment
model:

> Coping efforts are made in response to stressful apprais-
> als that signal harm or loss, threat, or challenge. Harm
> or loss refers to damage that has already occurred,
> threat refers to harm or loss that has not yet occurred
> but is anticipated, and challenge refers to an anticipated
> opportunity for mastery or gain. If the coping efforts
> that are initiated in response to a stressful appraisal
> change the relationship between the person and the
> environment by altering the situation and/or by changing
> the person's feelings about it, new appraisals or reap-
> praisals are made which in turn engender new coping
> efforts and so on (Folkman 1982, p. 97).

In this dynamic process, the person and the environment
are interdependent, each influencing and in turn being
influenced by the other. Thus, the environment acts upon
the person, who in turn acts upon the environment, which
acts upon the person, and so on.

The differences in meaning between adaptation, coping,
mastery, and defenses are confused (White 1974). Adaptation refers to the process of developing automatic patterns
that take over mindlessly when stressful events occur. Life
revolves around daily events that were once stressful but
now are not so because of the process of adaptation. Coping refers to the mechanisms that help one through an
event to which he has not adapted. Coping is not a mind-
less process; it involves conscious efforts on the part of the
individual under stress (White 1974). The first-year law
student, for example, is often said to be under extreme
stress and thus uses various coping mechanisms, but the
stress of the first year seems to lessen somewhat as the
student adapts during the second and third years. Coping
refers to psychosocial mechanisms that are used when

normal adaptive measures do not work. A main focus of this monograph is on coping rather than adaptation.

Lazarus, Averill, and Opton's definition of coping (1974) reflects White's distinction between coping and adaptation. Coping is "problem-solving efforts made by an individual when the demands he faces are highly relevant to his welfare (that is a situation of considerable jeopardy or promise) and when these demands tax his adaptive resources" (Lazarus, Averill, and Opton 1974, p. 250). Essentially, coping is used to help actualize some promise associated with the challenge of positive stress or to take the individual out of jeopardy when threatened with distress.

Individuals use both problem-focused and emotion-focused coping (Folkman 1982). Subjects in Folkman's study almost always used both types of coping, but the way in which the stressor was appraised affected the degree to which one type was used over the other. Individuals who saw the stressful situation as overwhelming were more likely to use emotion-focused coping, and as such their coping consisted mainly of regulating their emotional responses to the problem. If the individuals thought that the situation was manageable, however, they were more likely to use problem-focused coping to directly alter the source of stress. Problem-focused and emotion-focused coping can facilitate or impede each other (Folkman 1982)—the case with the student who minimizes the significance of a test (emotion-focused coping) and does not study adequately (problem-focused coping). Folkman's basic classification of problem- and emotion-focused coping is similar to Mechanic's earlier ideas about coping (1978), but perhaps her most important contribution is not that she developed a classification system but that she supported her system with research.

Stress and coping compose a complex within the person-environment model. The boundaries between stress and coping become blurred such that the way in which individuals cope can produce stress and even affect the stressor itself. For example, the stressful event first evokes a response on the part of the individual (see figure 1). This response involves both feelings (depression, anxiety, fear, excitement, for example) and an appraisal of the stressor. Second, the individual reacts to these initial evocative

FIGURE 1
STRESS-COPING COMPLEX

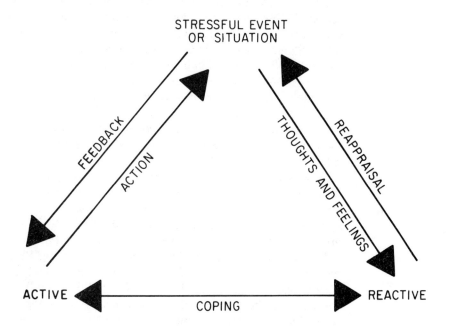

responses by using emotion-focused coping to regulate the
response to the stressful event. Regulating one's own
emotions does not directly change the stressful event itself.
For example, if a student is upset about failing a test, he or
she might cope by exercising, going to a movie, drinking
excessively, and/or giving oneself a pep talk. Although
these methods of coping will usually facilitate the individual's reappraisal of the stressor, they do not directly
change the stressor itself. The way in which one copes
with one's own reactions, however, affects the thoughts
and behaviors associated with the more active or direct
way of coping with the stressor. The third part of the
complex is the active or problem-focused coping; it can
include effective study methods, talking to a professor
about retaking a test, or withdrawing from a class. After
initiating such actions, the individual will likely receive
feedback about the consequences. The stress-coping complex incorporates the person-environment model because
the person and the stressor constantly affect each other.

Demographic variables as well as personal characteristics influence how an individual appraises stressful situations and copes with them. Three specific demographic variables influence students: race, sex, and marital status.

At all levels of higher education, race can be a critical factor when minority students enter programs previously denied to them. The potential for stress is further increased if minority students lack traditional academic preparation and minority faculty as role models.

Sex is a critical factor when men or women enter a field where they previously had been underrepresented—for example, women in law and men in nursing. Bias exhibited by faculty and other students may contribute to students' stress. As with minority students, the lack of role models in the faculty may decrease the chance of student-mentor relationships.

Marriage can be a positive or negative factor in stress among students. For some married students, support from one's spouse can provide additional social support. For others, schooling can negatively affect the marriage or vice versa. The likelihood of negative impact is increased when students see their role as student as childlike, in contrast to their role as spouse and possibly parent as adult.

Potential Effects of Stress on Students
By definition, being a student means experiencing stress. Ideally, a student will experience stress as a challenge and be left with a sense of competency, hope, and an increased capacity to learn, but many students experience distress, in which the threat of the educational process elicits helplessness and a forboding sense of loss. Further, the developmental context in which young students find themselves can add increasing levels of stress. Seven developmental vectors operate in the university student's life: achieving competency, managing emotions, becoming autonomous, establishing an identity, freeing interpersonal relationships, clarifying purpose, and developing integrity (Chickering 1969). Therefore, being a student means one is experiencing a great deal of developmental transition and change; these changes affect attitudes, interests, values, aspirations, and intellectual abilities more frequently for students than for nonstudents of the same age (Chickering 1969).

A crucial issue concerning distress among students is its effect on performance and learning. Most of the research concerning the effects of stress on cognitive abilities has been accomplished in a laboratory setting with a tightly controlled design (Hockey 1979). Perhaps the major exception is the vast amount of research that has validated the Yerkes-Dodson law, which demonstrates that high or low stress produces the poorest performers. (One study (Silver 1968) showed that law students described as low or high in relation to levels of anxiety performed more poorly than those whose levels of anxiety were described as midlevel).

Although studies supporting the Yerkes-Dodson law show that distress is harmful to performance, this law does not help one understand exactly what students do when they are under stress that contributes to poor performance. The research to date is inadequate in looking directly at specific behaviors that relate stress to performance among students. One way of understanding how stress might relate to students' performance is to look at the literature that focuses on cognitive problems in relation to stress and decision making. Another way to understand this issue is to look at the literature on human performance.

Premature closure . . . is [a] consequence of high stress in decision making.

Hypervigilance adversely affects cognitive functioning and decision making (Janis 1982). Hypervigilance, similar to **Selye's alarm** reaction, refers to excessive alertness to all signs of potential threat; it thus results in a diffusion of attention. When individuals become hypervigilant, they feel panicked and as a result become cognitively inefficient. Turow (1977) describes a first-year law student who panics about a test and spends hour after hour obsessively studying minute details and even reading material that is peripherally related to the course of study. Panicked students are not able to focus on the most important issues in the course and thus perform poorly on exams. Hypervigilance is characterized by a strong motivation to engage in a thorough search and appraisal, but continued threats become diversions that make attentiveness to the task of studying indiscriminate.

Premature closure (that is, quickly choosing a solution to end a stressful situation—perhaps by rushing through an exam) is another consequence of high stress in decision making (Janis 1982). The disadvantage of premature closure is that one's problem-solving abilities are diminished because alternative solutions are not generated. The student, more than the nonstudent, is faced with both social and intellectual transition (Chickering 1969); these transitions might create dilemmas that could put students in particular at risk of premature closure. Thus, it is possible that a student appearing poorly prepared for a test because he responded with superficial answers might be experiencing a high degree of stress that manifests itself with premature closure.

Although the extra attentiveness associated with hypervigilance seems to be opposite the superficiality associated with premature closure, it is not too difficult to imagine how both problems could (but not necessarily) occur together to adversely affect students' performance. For example, the obsessive student who is threatened by course material and becomes hypervigilant might not have the cognitive ability to integrate ideas in any meaningful way. This lack of integration might lead to premature closure in which only a small and perhaps superficial part of the material is displayed on a test. This example also reflects the narrowing of attention and the task-irrelevant behavior that is associated with high stress (Janis 1982).

Prolonged exposure to environmental stressors and/or to information overload results in cognitive fatigue—an insufficient reserve of attention to perform demanding tasks (Cohen 1980). Negative aftereffects on performance are magnified when the individual does not feel in control of the stressor.

Stress also results in some social aftereffects (Cohen 1980). Exposure to unpredictable and uncontrollable stress leads to decreased sensitivity to others—decreases in helping, decreases in recognition of individual differences, and increases in aggression. These social effects would at least indirectly diminish students' performance to the degree that an adequate support system helps mediate stress (Cobb 1976).

A fundamental assumption in Chickering's book (1969) is that "colleges and universities will be educationally effective only if they reach students 'where they live,' only if they connect significantly with those concerns of central importance to the students" (p. 3). One concept that can help students deal with stress is "stress inoculation" (Meichenbaum 1977). Stress inoculation is used to protect individuals from the disruptive and demoralizing effects associated with decisions that have a high potential for negative consequences. When using stress inoculation, the student first receives information describing what it is like to experience the negative consequences and how some consequences can be avoided. Merely receiving information about a stressful event has the effect of reducing stress because the individual is better able to mobilize resources in preparation for the event. For example, during an orientation for first-year law students, the subtle and intimidating "games" students play with each other to gain a competitive edge were vividly described. Merely exposing destructive games probably helped students to recognize them for what they are and thus helped eliminate the intimidating effects. In fact, such an approach would make it difficult for a student to seriously play the games if he knows that other students would recognize what he is doing.

Meichenbaum's stress inoculation training program (1977) incorporates information giving by first describing the nature of stress reactions to help individuals conceptualize them. Second, individuals actually rehearse how they would use coping skills. Third, individuals act out the newly learned skills in role plays and/or practice them in actual situations. A similar approach is used with new physicians beginning a residency program; videotaped vignettes of destructive interactions between new physicians and various health care professionals are shown to help anticipate effective coping.

Part of a stress inoculation program involves faculty members' being as specific as possible about the expectations of the programs and courses they teach. A forum where older students share experiences about how they coped and where the ins and outs of the educational program are described can help inoculate students against severe stress. Stress inoculation helps students feel in control and thus reduce the unpleasantness of the situation.

An effective stress inoculation program could be compared to an astronaut's preparation for space flight. Before their first liftoff into space, astronauts experience numerous simulated liftoffs and space trips in which they are faced over and over with a wide variety of possible threatening problems. Thus, during their first trip into space, they are so prepared for almost any dangerous situation that their responses to these situations are automatic. When students can anticipate and have some idea about how to control problems they have never encountered, they are better prepared to cope with stress. They will then be better able to focus their energies on the promises the educational process holds rather than the potential jeopardies.

COLLEGE STUDENTS

Environmental Setting

Stress is a product of interaction between an individual and the environment. Therefore, before looking at the nature of stress among college students, it is helpful to consider briefly the college environment. While many are aware that the first college in what would become the United States was Harvard, fewer know that before the end of its second year, the college closed when students' complaints of beatings and poor food forced the resignation of the first master of the new college (Lockmiller 1969). This incident suggests not that students' hardships characterize the history of American higher education but that, while some sources of stress are related to conditions of their times, stress also can be understood in the nature of colleges and institutions. In other words, stress among students occurs in the context of traditions (historical) and conditions (contemporary). "What our colleges do, tends either to be governed by tradition or to be improvised in the face of diverse—usually unanticipated—pressures" (Sanford 1967a, p. 1).

The aim of *The American College,* a multiauthored volume, was to sum up what was known of the effects on students of going to college. In the preface to the 1967 edition, Sanford noted that, since the book was first published in 1962, the Free Speech Movement had occurred at the Berkeley campus of the University of California. Because *The American College* "took up cudgels on behalf of the individual student and his development before campus unrest began to be widely noted," Sanford characterized the volume as "an analysis of what all the shooting has been about" (1967a, p. vii).

Ironically, Clark Kerr, the president where "all the shooting" took place, already had written an insightful book about changes that precipitated student unrest. In *The Uses of the University* (1963), Kerr observed that, because of the importance of knowledge to national economic and social growth, the nature and quality of the university has been reshaped. "Old concepts of faculty-student relations, of research, of faculty-administration roles are being changed at a rate without parallel" (p. vii). Kerr coined the term "multiversity" to describe the emergence of large, multipurpose institutions:

The University started as a single community—a community of masters and students. It may even be said to have had a soul in the sense of central animating principle. Today the large American university is, rather, a whole series of communities (p. 1).

Smith and Bernstein (1979), describing Kerr's multiversity as a "multiunit university," asked whether bigger is better: "Do they [organizations] become enervated when they expand past a certain point? In particular, do colleges and universities function poorly as learning communities when they become very large? We believe the answer often is yes" (p. 2).

Some statistics dramatize the accelerated growth of higher education since World War II:

- From 1959 to 1974, total enrollment increased 300 percent.
- In 1950, 75 percent of students were enrolled in colleges and universities with fewer than 2,000 students; by 1974, only 30 percent were enrolled in such institutions.
- In 1950, only 10 institutions enrolled more than 20,000 students; in 1974, there were 95 such institutions (Smith and Bernstein 1979, p. 2).

Increases in institutional size negatively affect students' personal development, with fewer opportunities to participate in extracurricular activities and to work closely with faculty (Smith and Bernstein 1979, p. 17). Personal values change. Levels of cheating increase with the size of a school; students at large institutions feel relatively anonymous in relation to the student body as a whole and feel less responsibility for upholding community values (Bowers 1964). While showing concern for colleges that "are too small to be effective in the use of their resources or in the breadth of the program they offer their students," the Carnegie Commission on Higher Education also decries the "cult of gigantism" (1971). The costs of bigness include:

- loss of personal attention to students
- loss of personal acquaintance among faculty members

- increase in administrative complexity
- increase in disruptive events on campus
- loss of the chance to serve new areas with new campuses
- loss of the chance to diversify with new and different types of campuses (p. 6).

Of course, not all colleges are large. Yet "university colleges" that are part of a university with big graduate programs, such as Yale or Michigan, or are administratively independent, such as Amherst, Oberlin, or Vassar, provide a *model* that other colleges regard as desirable:

> *Drawn by emulation on one side and pushed by accrediting agencies on the other, an increasing number of terminal colleges hire Ph.D.s from the leading graduate schools even though they fear the impact of men who may not be happy or complacent at a terminal college, and who may also make others less happy or complacent* (Jencks and Riesman 1969, p. 25).

In addition to accelerating size and to the emulation of growing institutions by other institutions, the environmental setting includes an increased diversity in the types of students seeking a college education.

> *Higher education in the United States until about 1940 was largely for the elite; from 1940 to 1970, we moved to mass higher education; and from 1970 to 2000, we will move to universal-access higher education—opening it to more elements of society than ever before* (Carnegie Commission 1971, p. 9).

Higher education in the United States is a "mosaic of differing institutions, goals, standards, and attitudes. . . . It is diverse, complex, and subject to rapid change" (Lockmiller 1969, p. 1). Stress is predictable in such an environment:

> *Given the diversity among students and the increasing size and complexity of the university campus, it is likely that many students are far from discovering the opti-*

mum conditions for themselves, or their campuses. . . .
Stress is seen as the consequence of an inadequate fit of
student needs and goals with the college environment
(Falk 1975, p. 27).

Within the context of diverse students with differing
needs coping with complex institutions, current environmental factors that may exacerbate stress include the rise
in college expenses, increased competition to get into
graduate and professional school, and an uncertain job
market for college graduates. "Time, money, [and] grade
point averages lurk like closet monsters for these youths,
threatening to snatch away chances they know they need
to become what they are capable of being" (DeMille 1983,
p. 71).

Sources of Stress
A theme of this monograph is that stress among students is
rooted in the past and the present. In other words, there
are both continuities and discontinuities. The continuity of
stress has occurred not just over decades, but over centuries (Katz 1975). This continuity of stress is rooted in the
inherent challenges colleges pose to incoming high school
graduates. The discontinuity of stress—that is, new conditions—includes student activism in the 1960s and cynicism
regarding change in the 1970s (Katz 1975, pp. 248–49).
Although current conditions can exacerbate student stress,
the basis for stress is rooted in the challenges colleges have
always posed for students. For many students, college is
an abrupt change from high school. The college years bring
separation from home and parents, academic demands are
greater than those in high school, and students face questions about personal identity and career choice. Some
authors emphasize the importance of the first two months
of college (Walker and Beach 1976); others warn of the
"sophomore slump," which occurs in the spring semester of the freshman year when freshmen "expect so much
and get so little" (Schoonmaker 1971, p. 103). Regardless
of when peak moments occur, all four years of college
can be viewed as a period of transition and change. To a
great extent, college poses a major challenge in an individual's life.

With challenge comes the promise of jeopardy. The potential for reward or punishment is great, depending upon success or failure.

> *The picture that emerges from our four-year study of college students is that of a wide variety of patterns in which individuals react and develop during the college years. The college environment is a highly controlling one, and it creates stress in many students. Some individuals are well enough equipped psychologically to utilize both the opportunities and the obstacles of the college environment for the purpose of their own growth. At the other end of the spectrum are those whose needs for passivity—for being told what to do—have become so much a part of their lifestyle that they do not experience the conditions of the environment as stressful or inhibiting. In between are the bulk of students, whose lives never reach an adequate self-awareness and . . . whose demands and constraints discourage their spontaneity* (Katz et al. 1969, p. 3).

Most educators have recognized that stress is necessary for growth. The problem has been to provide an optimum level of stress. The differences between "good stress" and "bad stress" have been recognized (Sherburne 1966, p. 343). Some educators have seen the need for psychiatric help as evidence of "bad stress." An early study of student psychiatric problems reported on the class that entered the University of Berkeley in the fall of 1961 as freshmen (Ellis 1969). Of the 3,474 entering students, 493 (14 percent) used the psychiatric clinic at the student health service over a four-year period. It would be simplistic to say that the institution caused these students' problems, as almost half of them reported previous counseling or psychotherapy. Nevertheless, their reasons for seeking psychiatric help at Berkeley portray a general picture of stress: depression, inability to do school work, nervousness, anxiety, and so on.

Another measure of stress is the college dropout rate. Again, while assignment of "cause" seems pointless, if not impossible, dropping out must be seen as the fleeing side of the "fight or flight" formula. In another study of Berkeley

Factors that may exacerbate stress include the rise in college expenses, increased competition . . . and an uncertain job market.

students, 9 percent of an entering class left and returned to school, and 50 percent left and did not return (Katz et al. 1969). In a review of the literature, under 50 percent of entering freshmen students nationwide finished college four years later (Hirsch and Keniston 1970). The decision to leave college was a crisis—"a moment of intensified anxiety and stress, a turning point, and the culmination of a long process of reflection and growing dissatisfaction" (Hirsch and Keniston 1970, p. 4).

College dropouts have been described as students who, in the face of environmental challenges, chose to change neither themselves nor the environment (Falk 1975). Rather, they chose to increase the distance between themselves and the source of stress, the college environment. Again, the image of college dropouts evokes "fight or flight," with flight being the chosen strategy. The "interactional stress" model of students' characteristics and environmental features has some support (Falk 1975). Stress is the consequence of a "mismatch" between student and college, but more systematic and quantitative research is needed to articulate the dynamics of the interaction between students and the college environment (Falk 1975). No satisfactory answer has yet been found to the question of what is the optimum rate of development for college students (Sanford 1967b, p. 55). Students "develop when stress is great enough to challenge their prior modes of adaptation, but not so great as to induce defensive reactions," but "how much stress does each student need?" (Sanford 1967b, p. 52). Unfortunately, no one has yet answered that question.

It is difficult to specify the sources of stress for college students because they comprise a diverse group located at diverse institutions. However, 50 percent of the college students who seek counseling complain of difficulty studying or of anxiety, tension, and depression related to poor grades or fear of doing poorly in courses (Blaine and McArthur 1971, p. 163).

Solutions
The reduction of stress in college students begins with their taking more control over their college education. Walker and Beach (1976), writing primarily for minority students, recommend that, in getting ready for college, students

figure out what to expect. Indeed, they offer a range of social, personal, and academic factors incoming students must consider:

- a feeling of greater isolation in college than in high school
- a greater variety of social and economic backgrounds in fellow students than was true in high school classmates
- a much greater variety of class size and teaching styles in college than in high school
- a tendency to base grades more on written work than on class performance
- greater personal responsibility for allocating time
- more competition in college than in high school
- less feedback about progress than in high school (p. 94).

This identification of differences and similarities between high school and college is a form of the stress inoculation described earlier. It is a way for students to gain control over their environment.

The lack of feedback, the last item on Walker and Beach's list, is an important factor because feeling in control is influenced by both information and feedback. Infrequent information about how students are doing may indicate a lack of feedback to students. A solution is to provide freshmen with midsemester grades.

A sense of control comes as students become independent:

The independent person makes his own decisions and controls his own life. He understands the world he lives in and knows what he wants from it. He can distinguish between important and trivial issues, and does not squander his time or energy on meaningless, self-destructive protests about trivialities (Schoonmaker 1971, p. 17).

To become independent, college students should analyze themselves, analyze "the system," and "take what we can offer" (Schoonmaker 1971, p. 20). That approach can be summarized as "help us help you" (p. 22). It fits well into the person-environment model, addressing the source of stress identified by Falk: a poor match between student and college. The solution is for students to work out a relationship with the system that helps them define themselves and reach their own goals (Schoonmaker 1971; Walker and Beach 1976).

A different approach—"let us help you"—is to provide mental health services for college students (Blaine and McArthur 1971).

> We are agreed, educator and psychiatrist alike, that the college should not be turned into a sanitarium. Nevertheless, attention must be paid to the feelings as well as intellects of people in education, if the college experience is to count as a major factor. . . . During the past twenty-five years or so, we have come to learn that the emotional climate of a school has profound implications for the effectiveness of the education it offers (Farnsworth and Munter 1971, p. 2).

Other helpers have other roles. The role of the college psychologist, for example, is changing from "a mental tester whose armamentarium consisted of a few intelligence tests" to someone whose practices "include assessment of intellectual functioning, the assessment of personality, diagnosis, therapy, guidance, and personnel assessment" (McArthur and Dinklage 1971, p. 28). Faculty have a role in counseling and referral: "The essential duty of the teacher who is attempting to help a student is to be a sympathetic listener" (Dalrymple 1971, p. 19).

A third approach to reducing stress is "help yourself by helping other students." College students themselves make excellent peer counselors, "promoting their own adaptation to college in the context of helping others" (Giddan and Austin 1982, p. ix). For example, the Telephone Counseling Service at Florida State University offers three major types of services: (1) information—for example, how to drop a course; (2) crisis intervention counseling by trained volunteers; and (3) referrals to campus and community agencies for problems that could not be resolved by a single telephone call (Kalafat and Schulman 1982). Other self-help programs at Florida State University include a multimedia career guidance program, a campus drug information center, and a student-operated academic advising service. Whatever the program, however, certain steps are necessary to make peer programs work: defining the needs, identifying the administration's and students' perspectives, and planning program evaluation at the start.

A variation of the self-help approach is a program at San Jose State College in which freshmen were recruited into "tribes" and "clans" (Finney 1975). A tribe of 80 students met monthly as part of some extra social activity and at two weekend marathons each semester. Each clan of 10 students met twice a week to discuss school. Based on a questionnaire, students in the program felt that their participation helped them handle their own problems.

A unifying theme is clear among these three approaches to reducing stress in college. Attempts to prevent or minimize distress focus on giving students a greater feeling of control over their campus environment. Information, feedback, and social support are essential ingredients.

GRADUATE STUDENTS

Environmental Setting

Although Yale graduated the first Ph.D. in 1861, most educators mark the official beginning of graduate education at Johns Hopkins University in 1876. The founding of Johns Hopkins is worth reviewing because it helped to shape the position that graduate students still hold today.

Johns Hopkins was a wealthy Baltimore merchant who made his fortune from the B&O Railroad. He provided in his will for the establishment of a new university and left the details to a board of trustees, who visited other universities and brought consultants to Baltimore. What they learned was that the last thing America needed was another college. They also learned that the best person to build up an institution quite different from a college was Daniel Coit Gilman. Gilman had been president of the University of California since 1872, where the trustees frustrated his attempt to build a new type of institution. By bringing Gilman to Johns Hopkins, the trustees demonstrated their desire that Johns Hopkins become an addition to American higher education rather than a rival to existing institutions (Gilman 1961; Rudolph 1962).

The model for graduate education at Johns Hopkins was the German university, with its emphasis on research. Thus, Johns Hopkins developed as a faculty-centered institution, where students provided the teachers with stimulation—the opposite of the traditional English college model, where teachers were theoretically engaged in the stimulation of students (Rudolph 1962).

While many American educators welcomed the doctoral degree, philosopher-psychologist William James wrote a famous essay in 1903, "The Ph.D. Octopus," in which he criticized the national movement toward the Ph.D. and its effects on his own institution, Harvard. Although most universities did not go so far as Johns Hopkins in its emphasis on faculty, the collegiate tradition was altered as institutions added graduate studies. Thus, American universities were founded on two different national patterns—a German university model for graduate study superimposed on the English college that had been the model for American undergraduate education—and "the resulting strain has characterized American higher education ever since" (Hartnett and Katz 1976, p. 6).

This strain has been a source of stress for both college and graduate students. On the one hand, college students learn that many faculty find their rewards in research rather than in teaching. On the other hand, graduate students learn that, when faculty do emphasize teaching, often it is done to accommodate undergraduate rather than graduate students.

In addition to the historical strain on graduate students resulting from the hybrid nature of American universities, two trends in American graduate education in the 1960s provided an additional source of stress for graduate students. First, during the 1960s the production of Ph.D.s nearly tripled.

Going to graduate school, an event which was typically received with a mixture of astonishment and admiration as recently as the 1950's, increasingly became an almost expected next step for many college seniors during the halcyon days of the sixties (Hartnett and Katz 1976, p. 8).

In addition to more individuals seeking doctoral degrees, more institutions began to offer doctoral degrees.

Along with the increase in graduate students, a second and related trend in the 1960s was the growth in federal funding. By the late 1960s, many graduate students were being supported by government funds. Together, these two trends of growth in numbers of students and in financial support by the federal government have made the graduate experience increasingly impersonal:

Many academic departments, which began as small, intimate groups of scholars with mutual concerns and interests, blossomed into large collections of diverse individuals. . . . Furthermore, the increased levels of federal funding created a vicious circle all its own. The grant money made expansion possible to be sure, but the newly acquired faculty then needed to obtain more money for support and further expansion. . . . At the same time—and most likely as a consequence—concern for students was neither respected nor rewarded (Hartnett and Katz 1976, p. 11).

Growth in numbers of students and in [federal aid] . . . have made the graduate experience increasingly impersonal.

In addition to the historical strain on graduate education and the pressures provided by growth and expansion in the 1960s, the environment of graduate education has posed further challenges in the 1970s and 1980s—the oversupply of Ph.D.s and the scarcity of job opportunities. Most academic leaders did not anticipate this trend (Mayhew 1970). Campus visits and interviews, an examination of planning documents, and questionnaires resulted in an "impressionistic interpretation" that:

> . . . emerges [as] a picture of graduate and professional education in which enrollments, problems, costs, and hoped-for-significance are expanding rapidly. . . . Those responsible for the expansion believe that they are responding to clear demands for professional manpower, for research and for service . . . and further that in some way or other the society will provide the necessary **financial support. What also emerges is considerable preoccupation with status, prestige, and growth at** institutions seeking to expand graduate and research capabilities, even if this should mean neglect of other educational values (Mayhew 1970, p. x).

Unfortunately, not only did most educators not foresee the oversupply of doctoral candidates and the lessened demand for doctoral graduates, the response to these changes has been slow. Most graduate departments have not stimulated many major program changes (Breneman 1975).

Mayhew (1970) distinguished "developing" from "developed" institutions. Developing institutions in particular, while hoping for increased federal support, were inclined to assume that state appropriations would provide not only for educational programs but also for faculty research (p. 3). Not surprisingly, the impact of poor employment opportunities and reduced federal support for graduate students has most affected the less prestigious departments, usually located in poorly financed private universities and in the lesser known institutions (Breneman 1975).

The environmental setting a graduate student enters today is at a crossroads:

After nearly a century of vigorous growth and expan-
sion, after a decade of generous treatment from federal
grant agencies, and after years of being viewed with
admiration and awe by large segments of the American
society—both for what it did for society at large and the
individuals who passed through its laboratories, li-
braries, and seminar rooms—graduate education has
arrived at a new point in its history. A creative and
imaginative response is clearly needed to insure the
long-range future and viability of American graduate
education (Hartnett and Katz 1976, p. 14).

What are graduate students supposed to accomplish in
this environmental setting? They are in the university
primarily to earn advanced degrees. They take courses,
write research papers, and fulfill other departmental obligations. After passing required preliminary examinations,
doctoral candidates write a dissertation. In most cases,
these tasks are very difficult. Why are graduate students
willing to undertake them?

What James and other critics predicted at the beginning
of the century has in substantial measure come about:
the tentacles of the "octopus" have reached out and
caught all too many whose sole reason for subjecting
themselves to the discipline of the Ph.D. is the prestige
endowed on the job made certain (Nisbet 1979, p. 516).

Within this milieu, it is not surprising that many graduate
students experience stress.

Sources of Stress
Although the oversupply of Ph.D.s and the discouraging
job market may be recent sources of stress for graduate
students, other sources probably are not different from
those experienced by graduate students a generation ago.
Sources of stress for graduate students are inherent in the
university environment, although current social changes,
such as an unstable economy, might complicate one's
coping with the stress (Altbach 1970; Halleck 1976; Valdez 1982).

Five conditions of graduate student life cause "friction, disaffection, and general unhappiness":

1. *Graduate students are adults in every sense of the term but are often treated as children by their universities.*
2. *Graduate students are often woefully exploited by individual professors, departments and universities, by way of inadequate remuneration for work performed, work loads which almost preclude prompt completion of academic work, or occasional plagiarism by senior professors of students' original work.*
3. *Graduate students are subject to arbitrary treatment by professors, departments or institutions and have few means of resisting such treatment.*
4. *Graduate students are often almost totally dependent on their professors or department for a livelihood, for certification as a scholar, and possibly for future academic positions.*
5. *The role of a graduate student as a teaching or research colleague with a senior professor is often ambivalent* (Altbach 1970, p. 565).

While a number of positive factors are associated with graduate student life (for example, a strong subculture that often provides psychological support), on balance the graduate student lives and works in a state of substantial powerlessness. "It is into the student's academic performance that the ultimate feeling of powerlessness enters. For it is upon the judgment of senior faculty members that his career depends" (Altbach 1970, p. 565).

Because evaluation of a graduate student's work requires great discretion, particularly in judging a doctoral dissertation, "the vagaries of the decision-making process are a cause of substantial frustration and strain" (Altbach 1970, p. 567). "Even when the student has confidence in the criteria of judgment and in the honesty of the professors involved, it is still with a feeling of anxiety that he enters into academic relationships" (Altbach 1970, p. 576). When students lack faith in the fairness and reliability of the evaluation system, they may engage in strategies to beat the system as a way of coping with the situation—for example, "cultivating the good opinion of a professor by establishing some sort of personal relationship with him" (Sanford 1976, p. 23).

In addition to a sense of powerlessness, some graduate students experience a feeling of ambiguity in their role as teaching assistants. It too is a source of stress. The emergence of the "departmental insurgencies" by teaching assistants at Wisconsin is a source of stress that, while relating to a temporary phenomenon such as the student revolution in the late 1960s, may also be rooted in the nature of graduate education (Altbach 1970). For example, the role of teacher may be stressful because the rewards for graduate students, like their faculty, lie in research, not teaching. Graduate students have always been expected to teach, yet in most cases they have had no prior teaching experience and are given little or no guidance by their faculty.

In one case, a patient known as Carl had done fairly well in graduate school until he assumed the role of teaching assistant.

In his teaching role, he felt strange and nervous. Even standing up before a group and attempting to impart knowledge seemed to him to be pretentious and phony. He could not make demands on his students. He refused to evaluate them and could not accept the possibility that his own superior expertise put him in a somewhat different position than he was in as an undergraduate (Halleck 1976, p. 165).

Carl had been a political activist as an undergraduate, and Halleck found it difficult to determine whether Carl's problems with assuming responsibility as a teaching assistant were based on political ideology or on some underlying personal problem. In any case, "even the limited authority of the graduate position was for him quite stressful" (Halleck 1976, p. 165).

The value of this case study and of others is that a source of stress, although related to social conditions such as student militarism in the 1960s and the overproduction of Ph.D.s in the 1970s, may also be rooted in the nature of graduate education. For example, maladaptive behaviors can be traced to two timeless needs of graduate students: the need for meaningful activity and the need for intimacy (Halleck 1976). With regard to the search for meaningful activity, "many of the minor anxieties and depressions that bring graduate students to the psychiatrist seem to be related to a profound fear of loss of potentiality that the student relates to the processes of specialization" (Halleck 1976, p. 163). In other words, graduate study by its very nature requires the student to become a specialist—in some cases a subspecialist—in a field of study. By choosing one focus, graduate students by necessity must limit their inquiries. Choosing a specialized field of study is a difficult choice and is accompanied by uncertainty:

> *Graduate students today are aware of the rapid rate of technological change, the impact of new scientific discoveries, and the impact of the information explosion. They appreciate that whatever they learn today is likely to be obsolete tomorrow. They fear specialization and believe that it will isolate them from too many aspects of real life. The pursuit of excellence in one relatively limited area of human knowledge seems to be almost stifling and alienating in a world that is characterized by rapid change* (Halleck 1976, p. 163).

With regard to the need for intimacy, "dissolution of relationships is currently the primary cause of emotional disorders among graduate students . . ." (Halleck 1976, p. 167). Although issues of dating and mating are critical for most unmarried adults in their twenties, some problems are unique to graduate students. "To achieve intimacy with others, one must first have the opportunity to meet others in a climate that allows intimacy to develop" (Halleck 1976, p. 169). The following pattern is apparent: "Graduate students who work with only a few people and who are likely to see the same individuals day in and day out can find themselves easily rutted into an extremely isolated, lonely life" (Halleck 1976, p. 169).

Graduate school and individual careers put stress on personal relationships (Hartshorn 1976). The human drive for social intimacy is compromised in the lives of married graduate students. Because graduate studies can become an all-consuming endeavor, lack of communication and lack of recreation time can be major sources of dissatisfaction. Financial issues are a prominent concern for most married graduate students (Gilbert 1982).

The need for meaningful activity and social intimacy is made more difficult to fulfill when graduate students go to a new school for their graduate training—the case for most graduate students. When they arrive at their new campus, first-year graduate students are like freshmen. Their situation can be more difficult than that of freshmen, however, because there are no orientation and social activities to welcome them (Halleck 1976).

Starting graduate school involves many life changes in addition to moving to a new place. Valdez (1982) used the Holmes and Rahe Social Readjustment Rating Scale (SRRS) to study 33 first-year doctoral students at a school of social welfare in the northeast. The SRRS is an instrument that assigns life change units (LCUs) to life events that require adaptation or coping. Each life event is assigned a weight. For example, "death of a spouse" is assigned 100 LCUs, "minor violation of the law" 11 LCUs. In Valdez's study, the first-year graduate students were asked to respond in terms of their first three months of graduate school. According to the SRRS, a score of 300 indicates "major crisis." The mean score for the students in the Valdez study was 313. One-third of the students fell into the "major crisis" level; another third experienced "moderate crisis." Only two students were "below crisis" level.

Valdez's conclusion was that a considerable number of life events occur among first-year graduate students and that graduate students may as a result be undergoing considerable stress (1982, p. 36). This statement is by its nature conditional because every individual perceives life changes differently and responds to them differently. An event that is a "major crisis" for one person is "mild" for another. Nevertheless, regardless of how individuals view changes in their lives, educators should view the first year of graduate school as a period of extraordinary change.

Thus far, the picture of graduate students that has emerged is of adults who *may* feel:

- powerless because of their dependence on faculty members' judgments
- ambiguity about their role as teachers of undergraduate students

- thwarted in their need for meaningful activity because of the impersonal nature of their departments and the narrow focus of their studies
- frustrated in their need for social intimacy because of the difficulty of attracting and/or maintaining personal relationships and
- overwhelmed from the many changes in their lives, especially in the first year of graduate school.

In this milieu, graduate students experience specific situations as stressful; that is, certain predicaments evoke negative feelings like discomfort and anxiety and provoke task-oriented responses. In one study to identify these types of situations, Kjerulff and Wiggins (1976) asked a stratified random sample of graduate students from the Department of Psychology at the University of Illinois to describe stressful situations they had experienced since entering graduate school. In particular, they were asked to concentrate on situations that had led them to consider dropping out of graduate school. Ten males and five females responded, providing 18 different situations. The stressful situations, which the investigators organized into three categories (academic failure, interpersonal problems, and fate-failure) appear in table 1. The examples of situations imagined by these graduate students certainly underscore the potential for jeopardy. Even if these situations are not experienced by any particular graduate student, they at least provide a basis for worry.

A stressful event can become a distressful one (Kolko 1980, p. 12). Negative thoughts can follow a stressful event, resulting in negative emotional states and in potentially counterproductive behaviors (see table 2).

The preliminary examination for Ph.D. candidacy is another stressful situation for many graduate students. One student reported on his postexam worries as follows:

As time went on, my doubts began to increase more and more. . . . I became more and more pessimistic. I was quite sure I hadn't passed. It sort of reached the climax the day they made the decision. . . . I just couldn't go over to the building and wait for the results. So I came home and nobody was there and I sort of paced the floor a bit. Then (another student) came in and told me that

TABLE 1
STRESSFUL SITUATIONS

Academic Failure	Interpersonal Problems	Fate-Failure
You flunk qualifying exams.	A faculty member is angry with you for not analyzing his data during finals week.	You feel lost in graduate school and find it a drag.
You are asked to leave school because you are slow on your master's thesis.	Your faculty advisor makes arbitrary criticisms on your master's thesis.	You are afraid you and your mate will not be able to get jobs near each other after graduation.
You make a "D" in a graduate course.		
You're slow to think up an idea for a dissertation and want to stay in graduate school a fifth year, but the department cannot support you.	You are in a research group with someone you dislike intensely.	Your subjects are not showing up and you feel very uninterested and unenthusiastic about your study.
	Your faculty advisor tells you that you spend too much time trying to be a good teacher.	
You flub up a class presentation in graduate seminar.		You are unexpectedly pregnant.
Your faculty advisor criticizes your in-class discussion habits.	Your program chairman is a hostile, difficult person and you are considering leaving.	Your mate accepts a job offer elsewhere before you are finished with graduate school.
No one likes your idea for your dissertation and you feel hopeless.	Your research advisor is very distant and unhelpful.	

Source: Kjerulff and Wiggins 1976.

he had passed and I heard that (another student friend) had passed, and they began to persuade me to call up. I wouldn't call up and I was quite positive at the time that I had failed the whole business. I was very anxious and very upset. . . . Finally, about seven o'clock I decided to call up (a faculty member) and no one answered. So I went to the building around eight o'clock. I heard that

TABLE 2
AN EXAMPLE OF ACADEMIC STRESS

Situation

You have two weeks to prepare for an exam and to complete a written assignment. The week before you couldn't spend as much time on coursework as you needed because of research and/or your job. It's the first test and the first written assignment for each course, and you really wanted to do well on both.

Cognitions

1. It's only the beginning of the term and I'm already behind. How will I get caught up?

2. It will be terrible if I don't do well on this first assignment!

Feelings/Emotions

1. Dread working so hard over the next two weeks.

2. Afraid of doing poorly, apprehensive.

3. Angry that research/job had required so much time.

4. Frustrated that I didn't have more time to spend on coursework.

5. Despondent over possibility of failing at the beginning.

Behavior

1. Complain to friends and classmates about situation.

2. Stay up late worrying about performance.

3. Refuse several invitations for leisure activities to improve productivity.

4. Become irritable and short with people.

5. Begin looking for an alternative career.

Source: Kolko 1980.

he would be there. I was really completely shook up. It took about everything I could do just to walk up the stairs and go in. I was quite convinced that I had failed, and the thing that bothered me was that I tried rationalizing everything and saying that it really wasn't that important and that I could take it over again, and so forth. . . . The thing that bothered me more than anything else was I thought I had failed, but it was a question of how I could accept the failure (Mechanic 1978, p. 1).

Mechanic's study of how students perceived and responded to these exams was conducted in 1960, originally published in 1962, and republished in 1978 with a new foreword by the author. Not only was this study a breakthrough when it was conducted and reported; it remains the best qualitative study of how people come to feel stress and how they deal with it. In the study, 22 students agreed to participate (the three who refused gave pressures of time as their reason). During weekly and bimonthly interviews, including interviews, before and after the examination, Mechanic interviewed each student approximately 10 times. Four weeks before the examination, students and faculty completed questionnaires, and four weeks after the examination, students completed a questionnaire. Mechanic also occasionally interviewed faculty and spouses of students. He observed interactions in the department and attended a faculty meeting concerned with the examinations.

Based on this comprehensive qualitative collection of data, Mechanic found that *communication* was a key factor. Because students had no fully rational basis for preparing for the preliminary exam, they attempted to gauge their activities by observing each other. Through social comparison, students anticipated their own capability to prepare for the examinations and evaluated their own progress. A favorable comparison increased a student's confidence; an unfavorable one provoked a feeling of discomfort. Because communication could lead to both comfort and discomfort, therefore, students often communicated with caution.

When a student feels self-doubts . . . negative feelings can serve to handicap attempts at coping.

The major contribution of Mechanic's study is his description of the interplay between coping and defense mechanisms—that is, how people deal with the challenge and how they deal with their feelings about the challenge. For example, when a student feels self-doubts as a result of social comparison, negative feelings can serve to handicap attempts at coping like concentration and study. On the other hand, a student who feels too self-assured runs the risk of not harnessing enough energy to concentrate and study.

Thus, within the setting of graduate school, the graduate student is faced with a gamut of specific challenges. Of these challenges, the preliminary examination is perhaps the penultimate. Writing a doctoral dissertation is certainly the ultimate. Faced by a variety of difficult challenges, it is not surprising that many graduate students consider dropping out of school (Heiss 1970). Over one-third of the respondents to Heiss's questionnaire interrupted their studies or had been tempted to drop out of the doctoral program.

> *In most cases, students ascribed their doubts to pressures which demanded coping mechanisms other than those used to resolve academic problems. For the most part, the pressures generated self-doubts that debilitated the respondent's interests or caused him to question the wisdom of investing his energies in the demands of the "system"* (Heiss 1970, p. 177).

The specific reasons why graduate students were tempted to give up their quest of a Ph.D. are shown in table 3. These reasons are related to the categories in table 1. "Stress of passing hurdles" falls under the category "academic failure," "family problems" under "interpersonal problems," and "disillusionment with graduate education" under "fate-failure."

One estimate, difficult to substantiate, is that nearly 50 percent of the people who enter graduate school with intention to complete a doctoral degree never finish (Heiss 1970). Without knowing for certain what the rate of incompletion is nationwide, one can still infer that it is high. Although "doctoral candidates who never complete their dissertations, and therefore fail to earn the Ph.D., have not been a topic of much systematic study" (Jacks et al. 1983, p. 74), their reasons are again related to academic failure, interpersonal problems, and fate-failure (see table 4).

Another manifestation of distress among graduate students is the prevalence of emotional disorders. A review of records of the University of Wisconsin student psychiatry section found that graduate students were second only to freshmen in terms of using psychiatric services (Halleck 1976). "Efforts to establish the incidence of use of mental health facilities by graduate students at other universities revealed similar findings" (Halleck 1976, p. 161). An earlier report (Nelson 1971) also found that a high proportion of students requiring the use of Harvard's mental health unit were graduate students. Although approximately one-half of the students in Nelson's study (1971) had es-

TABLE 3
REASONS WHY GRADUATE STUDENTS WERE
TEMPTED TO DROP OUT

Reason	Percent*
Disillusionment with graduate education	44.4
Tired of study	40.5
Stress of passing hurdles	37.0
Faculty lack of interest in students	26.0
Lack of interest in field	25.2
Financial problems	22.5
Academic problems	16.0
Poor relationship with advisor	13.8
Family problems	12.2
Uncertainty about draft status	12.2
Health problems	6.3
Poor relationship with sponsor	5.9

*Percentages total more than 100 because individuals gave more than one example.
Source: Heiss 1970.

TABLE 4
REASONS FOR LEAVING DOCTORAL PROGRAMS

Reason	Percent*
Financial difficulties	44
Poor working relationship with advisor and/or committee	44
Substantive problems with research for the dissertation	36
Personal or emotional problems	36
Receipt of an attractive job offer	32
Interference of paid work with work on dissertation	28
Family demands	24
Lack of peer support	20
Loss of interest in earning a Ph.D.	12

*Percentages total more than 100 because individuals gave more than one example.
Source: Jacks et al. 1983.

tablished psychoneurotic symptoms, it is not possible to link the causes of these problems to distress in graduate school. In fact, students may have brought these problems with them to graduate school. Even so, approximately one-fourth of the students did not have well-established mental illness in the traditional sense, and their problems were "frequently related to specific and clearly seen circumstances" of graduate school (p. 321). One student, for example, ". . . felt socially inadequate and very concerned at his hesitation to develop warm relationships with women" (p. 322). In this case, his problems happened to stem from his family relationships, but the drive to fulfill the need for social intimacy requires a social setting that encourages companionship—something not commonly found in the graduate school environment.

The sources of stress for graduate students stem in part from an environmental setting that poses numerous challenges. In the face of these challenges, some students cope effectively and are strengthened by the experiences. Others do not cope as well and are distressed by graduate school. Given that many graduate students do not succeed, or they succeed but find the experience distressing, the challenge to administrators, faculty, and students is to develop graduate study "that encourages maturity and fosters 'a growing self-dignity and ripe poise' " (Nelson 1971, p. 333).

Solutions

Proposals to minimize stress should take into account that some stress is beneficial but that unnecessary stress is an impediment. "Some degree of stress is inescapable (in that it underlines to the student the importance of the course he is undertaking), but it seems only commonsense to take every possible step to cut out sources of needless anxiety" (Cleugh 1972, p. 86). Requirements for advanced degrees should be challenging yet achievable. While a basic theme of the literature is that needless distress can be prevented by providing students with appropriate levels of control, the numerous course requirements of many doctoral programs provide graduates with little control, particularly early in the program. "Most of the psychological stress and educational disillusionment resulting from too little independence seems to occur during the first year of gradu-

ate study, when many students are locked into a rigid
pattern of required courses and examinations (Heiss 1970,
p. 283). A graduate student agrees:

> *I ask you to think for a moment of the number of "re-*
> *quired" courses that are part of your program. Is it*
> *necessary, as graduate students, most of whom have*
> *had professional experience, to be supervised and*
> *steered through a program? Is there an opportunity to*
> *pursue those areas that we wish to pursue as graduate*
> *students, indeed is there any time left in our programs to*
> *do this? Do graduate students have an opportunity to*
> *participate in the planning of curriculums of higher*
> *education? Do we have the opportunity to express our*
> *feelings and concerns about the future of our field to*
> *those who will ultimately make curriculum and program*
> *decisions?* (Norman 1970, p. 1).

Both Heiss and Norman recommend that doctoral students
be allowed to play a greater role in designing their own
academic programs.

Related to the issue of control are the concepts of information, feedback, and predictability. "Lack of necessary
information and explanation, so that students feel themselves in the dark, is a potential cause of stress" (Cleugh
1972, p. 87). Entering graduate students can be assigned a
"buddy" before they arrive on campus to help provide
them with the information they need (Valdez 1982). Orientation activities for graduate students should be "no less
comprehensive than those for freshman undergraduates"
(Halleck 1976, p. 175).

Students also need feedback—information about current
performance that can be used to guide future performance—to feel in control. It is ironic that graduate programs
that use "pass-fail" grading to reduce anxiety may actually
be increasing it unless students receive some other form of
feedback as well. Small group conferences, colloquiums,
and informal meetings are possible settings where students
can receive information about the quality of their work
(Heiss 1970).

Graduate students tend to have two types of responses
to the tasks expected of them: "The gamesman attempts to
perform fewer tasks for more rewards, while the grind

performs all of the tasks expected of him for the rewards already promised" (Sanford 1976, p. 1). Based on interviews with 72 graduate students in the departments of chemistry, economics, and English at the University of California at Berkeley, Sanford found that "in extreme cases, both gamesmen and grinds may be unable to see how the system can be coped with by any means other than their own" (p. 1). The recommended solution is to discourage both extremes by increasing the flexibility in program requirements and evaluation methods so that graduate students feel they can cope by means other than "beating the system" or "grinding it out."

Feeling in control also requires feeling that what will be experienced in graduate school is predictable. But "a general belief [exists] among students that grading and evaluating are haphazard and mechanical" (Heiss 1970, p. 125), and graduate students sometimes feel that how their dissertation research will be judged is unpredictable (Altbach 1970).

One solution to lack of control and related shortcomings in information, feedback, and predictability is a more substantial role for the advisor in the graduate student's life. Advisors can contribute substantially to creating a positive environment for graduate students. They can provide "positive, nonverbal cues and overt expressions of interest in a student's welfare" as well as "open discussion of the developmental issues confronting a student" (Bargar and Mayo-Chamberlin 1983, p. 410). The advisor can help reduce the stress associated with the doctoral dissertation by helping the student articulate and assess alternatives so that he or she can develop the topic earlier in the program and by supporting the student during topic development, research, writing, and oral defense (Bargar and Mayo-Chamberlin 1983, p. 415).

The solutions for reducing distress among graduate students have focused thus far on the environment, for example by providing orientation for new students, by increasing students' involvement in planning, and by enhancing the role of advisors. Other solutions focus on improving the student's ability to cope with stress. Kolko (1980) recommends specific strategies for solving problems and managing time that "can be employed to facilitate one's adjustment to graduate school" (p. 9). Schoonmaker (1971) also addresses the issue of one's personal adjustment to graduate school. First, because graduate school is so demanding, he suggests that only students willing to make a complete commitment go. Once in graduate school, students should realize that after a few weeks many students think they are not intelligent enough to continue: "They experience a graduate-school version of the 'freshman jitters.' The work seems overwhelmingly difficult and their classmates seem to be much more intelligent than they are" (p. 286). Students feeling this stress should realize that other students, because of their own feelings of stress, engage in gamesmanship. Consequently, in their attempts to impress each other, graduate students become even more confused and frightened. Graduate students who start having doubts about their own abilities should not put up a front when they are not familiar with terms and authorities.

Admit your own ignorance because it is not stupidity; in fact, awareness of your ignorance is the first step toward overcoming it. You do not know these terms and authorities, nor do you need to know them now. You were accepted because you have the brains to hear them, and, if you have the courage to admit your ignorance, you will make much better use of the time that other people waste trying to impress each other (Schoonmaker 1971, p. 286).

Others advocate that professional counseling be made more available to graduate students. In fact, Nelson (1971) recommended that more therapeutic hours should be available for graduate students than for undergraduates. Better counseling services would help when "pain, anxiety, and pressure reach a point for many beyond any stress that might be justified as encouraging effort and productivity" (Katz and Hartnett 1976, p. 272).

Undoubtedly, solutions for distress will have to be tailored to the needs of individual departments and schools and the involvement of both faculty and students is necessary to formulate solutions. The impetus for change is present in both teacher and learner:

Anxiety states are frequently experienced by students in pursuit of graduate degrees. As professor of these stu-

dents we need to ask ourselves some hard, penetrating questions. What are the causes of anxiety expressed in the educational milieu? Can we differentiate between manifestations of anxiety that students must accept and live with from neurotic anxiety? What are the earmarks of non-productive anxiety-ridden behavior? Is the educational program contributing to the non-productive experiences? (Montgomery 1972, p. 24).

What all of this boils down to is that we must begin to assume responsibility for our present state of life. We must not, as all minorities have learned, wait for changes to be initiated from above or without. They will only occur from within. A very long time ago someone told me the definition of security *was the* freedom *to be and feel* insecure! *Perhaps we as graduate students should ponder this for awhile* (Norman 1970, p. 4).

LAW STUDENTS

Environmental Setting

The history of legal education follows the familiar pattern of other professions like medicine, nursing, and pharmacy. Before the turn of the century, lawyers trained primarily in apprenticeships, but by 1940 admission to the bar with few exceptions meant that one had to have three years of formal legal education. The specific way that the law profession and legal education developed historically helps one understand the cultivation of stress in law school.

During the colonial period, lawyers were viewed with suspicion and distrust. They were perceived as "mostly pettifoggers, or minor court officers such as deputy sheriffs, clerks, and justices who stirred up litigation for the sake of petty court fees" (Harno 1953, p. 18). This negative view began to change during the latter part of the 1700s, when predominately lawyers were involved in the writing of the Declaration of Independence and the Constitution. Legal education in the United States during the colonial period was desultory. In fact, because no courses of law were offered in colleges and there were no independent law schools, apprenticeships were the only form of training except for a few extremely scarce law books. During the end of the 1700s, as attitudes toward lawyers became more positive, the first efforts toward formal legal education arose when Thomas Jefferson founded a chair of law at William and Mary College (1779). Shortly afterward, various professorships of law were established at a number of colleges. The men who filled these teaching positions saw the practice of law as more than a craft and their role as that of developing statesmen (Harno 1953).

The Litchfield Massachusetts Law School, opened in 1794, was the first independent law school in the United States. During its 50 years of existence, the Litchfield School was never associated with a college; in fact, it was staffed by faculty who were all practicing attorneys. Its educational orientation was therefore practical rather than theoretical. One remarkable quality of the Litchfield School was that over 25 percent of the school's graduates became prominent national leaders. Numerous U.S. senators and representatives, cabinet members, governors, Supreme Court justices, and vice-presidents graduated from this school. Indeed, Litchfield provided a tremendous boost to the prestige of the legal profession.

A major setback in legal education occurred at Litchfield's zenith, however. In 1828, Andrew Jackson spearheaded the "new democracy," a movement that strongly deemphasized the need for formal education. With respect to the legal profession, "in its implication this creed seemed to hold that all male citizens had the inherent right to practice law" (Harno 1953, p. 39). Partly as a result of Jacksonian democracy, for several decades law schools were seen as merely peripheral and in fact unnecessary in the education of lawyers. During this period, for example, not only was Harvard Law School plagued with poor attendance, but in one year only four students enrolled even though the qualifications to enter were merely that the student be of good moral character and be at least 19 years of age. Throughout the mid-1800s, the prestige of the legal profession was again at a low point; it was not until the late nineteenth and early twentieth centuries that lasting and critical developments in formal legal education began to occur.

The transition of colleges to universities was concurrent with changes in the practice of law that profoundly affected legal education (Johnson 1978). Universities were not satisfied merely to train the individual in the craft of law; rather, they saw legal education as a scientific endeavor. At the same time, various bar associations were upset at the influx of immigrant lawyers. They viewed immigrant lawyers as poorly trained, of improper birth, ignoble (they advertised for business), creators of unnecessary litigation, and threats to both professional ethics and fundamental values of American life (Johnson 1978). A major concern of the elite members of the bar was to control economic competition. Bar associations saw legal education as a way to "cleanse" the profession, and, thus, practitioners who were trained under the apprentice system and originally viewed formal education as unnecessary began to support higher academic standards as a way to screen admission to the profession.

Harvard led the change in the 1870s by replacing faculty who were primarily practitioners with career law professors committed to the scientific study of law. This transition saw no systematic and sustained discussion on how best to teach young men and women in legal techniques and professional values, and so legal education developed as a piecemeal adjustment to academic changes and professional concerns (Johnson 1978). During the 1870s, Harvard's admissions requirements, curriculum, and teaching methods evolved and later became the standard for almost all law schools in the United States. Both the Socratic and the case methods were developed at Harvard in the 1870s; they are still commonly used in current legal education. The academic changes and professional concerns at that time led to a number of problems that are directly or indirectly associated with the stress that law students face today.

One problem is that the Socratic method puts the law professor in complete control of the classroom; the students' role is only to answer questions from the professor, not to ask any. Students have little control over how they relate to the material being taught in class. Second, legal education has become a screening instrument in the extreme because the most prestigious law firms choose their clerks almost exclusively from among the top 10 to 20 percent of the class. Third, career law professors come from the ranks of the most successful law students. The century-old methods of legal education are perpetuated by those who have been rewarded most by the system; therefore, changing legal education becomes less likely (Silver 1968). Fourth, efforts to make legal education more analytical and less craftlike mean that the practical aspects of law—that is, negotiating skills and courtroom practice—receive less emphasis. Second- and third-year law students, in particular, want more practical training and professors with practical experience (Pipkin 1976).

Sources of Stress
Compared to the amount of literature on stress among graduate and medical students, there is a dearth of material about stress and law students. Further, much of the material about law students is anecdotal; relatively few actual scientific studies have focused on the topic.

A comprehensive study of six law schools in the United States, however, found that students entered law school primarily because of an intrinsic interest in the subject and a desire for professional training and intellectual stimulation (Stevens 1973). According to this study, the extrinsic rewards of income and prestige were of less value to these students. In considering the sources of stress discussed in this section, one might ask first to what extent the intrinsic interest in the subject of law is discouraged or encouraged and whether students are left more challenged to learn as a result of the stress or discouraged and helpless and thus less interested in the intrinsic rewards. These questions are central to the issue of whether or not law schools provide an optimum atmosphere in which to learn.

The Socratic teaching method has been cited as a major source of stress among law students. When this teaching method is used, students receive little if any feedback to help evaluate their performance. The Socratic method openly emphasizes the competitive nature of law before the student has a chance to become familiar with the basic material to be learned (Silver 1968). The student is asked to answer the professor's questions and criticize the previous student's remarks and, because the professor rarely comments on a student's answers, the student often is left feeling that an answer was inadequate (Silver 1968). This teaching method encourages a great deal of hostility between students (Stone 1971). It creates problems with morale; the relatively quiet students tend to make disparaging comments to each other about those who seem to enjoy answering the professor's questions (Turow 1977). One-third of the students in one study actually felt degraded by the Socratic method of teaching (Stevens 1973); the method is more a source of frustration than of enlightenment (Silver 1968). One-third of the law students in another survey felt the Socratic method to be substantially or severely distressful (Ellinwood, Mayerson, and Paul 1983). One faculty member from the University of Utah Law School, however, maintains that over the past decade the use of the Socratic method has declined and no school currently uses it as the principal method of teaching.

Particularly related to the Socratic method are the concerns about feedback. Law students receive little or no feedback about their performance until after the first semester. A lack of feedback was a source of substantial or severe stress in 51 percent of the law students in one survey (Ellinwood, Mayerson, and Paul 1983). Out of a need to reduce the stress associated with little feedback, law students eventually develop their own methods of bogus feedback—what an individual develops in his own mind that generally has nothing to do with actual performance—that ultimately prove ineffective (Silver 1968).

Undue importance is placed on grades at the end of the first year of law school—partly because of a lack of earlier feedback. This undue pressure, however, is more likely the result of the fact that one's career opportunities as a lawyer are largely determined by the end of the first year, perhaps even as early as the end of the first semester. Generally, the top 10 percent of the class is given the opportunity to write for the school's law review, which is considered such a high honor that the most prestigious law firms actively recruit mainly those students. The students who do not "make law review" or who are not in the top 10 to 20 percent of their class are rarely invited to interview with prestigious firms. Law schools rarely help students in the lower ranks find interviews with less prestigious firms, corporations, or government agencies.

The stress related to grades can have a devastating effect on learning for some students.

The amount of pressure on grades is relatively unique to law school because in no other university setting do grades have the importance at such an early point in one's education. Of 17 potential items causing stress among law students in one survey, getting grades that did not reflect the amount of effort invested proved to be the most stressful item (Ellinwood, Mayerson, and Paul 1983). The second most stressful item was the importance placed on class rank. At least 60 percent of the students surveyed in that study felt substantial or severe levels of stress related to each of these two items.

This inordinate pressure for high grades, particularly in the first year, likely has a detrimental effect on learning and thus contributes to the sharp decline in intellectual interest in subsequent years (Stevens 1973). It is as though the students worked as hard as they could but discovered that getting the best grades was out of reach. The stress related to grades can have a devastating effect on learning for some students. One student who actively participated in class and seemed to offer insightful answers to professors' questions abruptly and permanently stopped classroom participation shortly after discovering that his performance on the exams was average (Turow 1977).

The stress associated with grades also is associated with ineffective study habits (Patton 1968). Patton asked those in his study to name what stood out most in any way about the first year in law school. The most common response referred to a feeling—being confused, afraid, or uncertain, for example. The students who were unable to overcome these distressful feelings were the ones who tended to have poor grades. Such students were found to study unsystematically and were unable to adjust to the differences in teaching methods between undergraduate education and law school. The poorer students tended to focus on answers to legal problems rather than on learning the process used to analyze legal issues; they focused on content rather than method. According to one student who performed poorly:

> *I don't know that I could put my finger on any one thing. I would say that the amount of work and the uncertainty with which I approached finals, not really knowing what I was expected to have and how well I was doing all along. In other words, there was no basis for me to compare myself with other students or compare myself on a scale of knowledge . . . with what I should have had* (Patton 1968, p. 29).

After the first semester, tension was related primarily to grades, with students who had the worst grades feeling the most tension (Stevens 1973).

Another source of stress is the distance students feel from the faculty. Although most university students likely share this same concern, unique qualities of legal education emphasize the differences between students and faculty (Watson 1968). It is not uncommon to find law professors who say that their teaching is directed primarily to the intellectually elite student or to those students in the top 10 percent of the class. Furthermore, although law professors might care for their students, they often feel unable to teach the majority effectively and so focus their efforts on those students who are most responsive to what they teach, failing to recognize the emotional cues of distress from the majority (Watson 1968). The psychological distance also occurs as a result of some professors' inappropriate brutality—openly insulting students and psychologically cutting them to ribbons. Some professors justify their behavior as preparation for the stress of the courtroom or for the stress of negotiating. In the adversarial environment of the legal world, however, the opposing attorney does not have the protection of being "the professor" who carries on a one-sided battle.

Law students cope with these sources of stress in different ways. Several ways they use to avoid stress likely have a deleterious effect on learning in law school (Stevens 1973). "Most interviewees felt that the prevalent teaching method not only discouraged student participation but also forced students to design avoidance tactics to allow the peaceful functioning of their personal learning mechanisms" (Stevens 1973, p. 644). Some of the avoidance tactics included not attending class, personally requesting the professor not to call on them, not returning to class after a break, making highly equivocal statements, and stating they were not prepared when in fact they were but feared answering questions. The most common means of avoidance, according to Stevens, was the statement, "I'm not prepared." Ironically, for many students the experience of law school encourages them to avoid and relinquish aggressive skills to feel comfortable with their learning environment (Watson 1968).

Perhaps in an effort to deal with their own sense of helplessness, many students rely on false feedback as confirmation that they will perform well on exams (Silver 1968). For example, some students believe that because they are older, married, make "good" comments in class, had a high LSAT score, or did well in their legal writing seminar (a nongraded exercise), they will rank high in the class. The extent to which students rely on such feedback to relieve their anxieties might be counterproductive and even harmful if they begin to avoid adequate preparation for exams.

The nature of coping seems to change dramatically for students after the first year when anxieties seem reduced. This change is perhaps partly the result of adapting to the environment or feeling a diminished commitment to do well in law school. If law students believe that their efforts are not a reflection of their grades, it is not hard to imagine how commitment to perform well could decrease. A random sample of students from seven law schools found an apparently cynical view of legal education from students in their last year:

On the average third year students reported that law was not taught in law school in a systematic and orderly fashion, that class attendance was unrelated to obtaining high grades, that cramming for exams was as effective as regular study, that case briefing was not an effective way to learn law, and that grades were given largely to aid firms in hiring rather than as feedback on progress (Pipkin 1976, p. 1173).

As law students begin to see their education in these terms, it is not surprising that they use avoidance techniques and become less committed to the process of learning. The adaptation to the stress of law school after the first year might to a large extent merely be resignation.

Solutions

From a historical perspective, legal education in the twentieth century developed in large part out of pressures to limit the number of people entering the practice of law. The extent to which the perceptions of students are true that grades are used primarily for hiring purposes rather than for feedback would lead one to conclude that the original purposes of legal education might still exist. To decrease cynicism and increase ambition, students must have the perception that the primary focus of education is learning rather than aiding firms in hiring.

Most authors who have studied stress in law school strongly recommend more frequent and useful feedback, which can be accomplished by:

- communicating with students about the meaning of grades
- assigning more frequent exams and papers and providing instruction in study techniques
- offering positive reinforcement by means other than grading—for example, by acknowledging a good question in class or by praising the class when students are prepared rather than chastising them only when they are ill prepared (Ellinwood, Mayerson, and Paul 1983, p. 28).

Pipkin (1976) asked students to rank the importance of 24 possible changes in law school and found that "more feedback on academic progress" (p. 1184) was ranked second after smaller classes.

Merely acknowledging the stress associated with the Socratic method will likely have the effect of reducing stress. But other recommendations regarding the method would likely reduce stress:

- professional education training for law faculty
- more organized progression through course material, following the syllabus
- less reliance on the traditional case book method (Ellinwood, Mayerson, and Paul 1983, p. 28).

Although Pipkin's subjects (1976) did not feel that the Socratic teaching method should change, they strongly recommended changes in the curriculum that would alter the prevalence of the Socratic method. Students asked for more focus on the teaching of practical skills and more faculty who had actual experience in the practice of law. Of 24 changes in legal education suggested, the third through sixth most recommended changes regarded helping students gain practical skills and plan careers (Pipkin 1976). It is likely that a more practical approach to training lawyers would often include methods other than Socratic teaching. Some law schools (Stanford and Harvard, for example) have recently developed programs to train students in negotiation and courtroom skills. Such training specifically acts as a form of stress inoculation before the actual practice of being an attorney.

If students believe that their efforts are not reflected in grades and that the current importance of grades adversely influences effective study techniques, then perhaps the importance of grades should be deemphasized. Other forms of feedback are likely more helpful in improving learning. The following suggestions would likely help deemphasize grades:

- stop posting grades; mail or distribute them individually
- stop ranking; issue grades only
- base selection for the law review more on writing skills[1]

[1] In fact, Stanford University recently implemented this practice.

- facilitate off-campus interviews at small law firms, public interest law practices, utilities, corporations, and government agencies (Ellinwood, Mayerson, and Paul 1983, pp. 28, 30).

As more effort is made to help find jobs for students who are not in the top 10 to 20 percent of the class, it is likely that the stress associated with high grades would be reduced.

Faculty who are supportive of students likely have a beneficial effect in reducing stress and even increasing learning. In fact, greater support from faculty has been more strongly associated with reducing stress than the support of one's family (Ellinwood, Mayerson, and Paul 1983). Warm and friendly relationships between faculty and students positively affect students' expectations and their sense of ambition (Stevens 1973). Approximately one-third of the students in Stevens's survey did not perceive their faculty as warm and cordial, and over one-third of the students in Ellinwood, Mayerson, and Paul's report felt substantial or severe stress because they were unable to establish rapport with faculty. In Stevens's survey, the perceived warmth of the student/faculty relationship was associated more strongly with ambition than was class rank, but ironically for many students, a high class rank opened the way to warmer relations with faculty. Rapport between students and faculty can be increased by:

- assigning each student a faculty advisor/friend— especially during the first year
- for the faculty, trying to communicate with students in ways other than just in the classroom
- organizing more student/faculty social events
- participating in events organized by students
- not focusing on law review students in class discussion (Ellinwood, Mayerson, and Paul 1983, p. 28).

Better relationships between students also help reduce stress. First-year students in one study who spent time associating with upper class students were much more relaxed and spent less time formally discussing course material than those students who did not have these associations (Stevens 1973). It is not known whether students' performance improved as a result of these associations. Even if it did not, however, the fact that the associations reduced stress means that it is worthwhile to increase informal contact between students in different classes.

In summary, students begin law school intrigued with law, but over three years their interest is greatly diminished. Law students' interest in law can be maintained if grades are deemphasized and if feedback is more relevant and timely. Improved relationships between faculty and students and increased practical learning and career planning will also help reduce stress and increase students' ambition to become attorneys. The concern is that the same historical compulsions that encouraged the development of formal legal education might still have an inordinate presence. Thus, law schools can still be under pressure to maintain the role of screening agents for law firms. Law students are quite cynical about the process and purpose of their education (Pipkin 1976). It is likely that, as legal education increasingly focuses on benefiting more than the top 20 percent of a class, both the cynicism and overwhelming distress will give way to an improved learning environment.

Environmental Setting

The entire process of medical education is often viewed as an 11- to 12-year continuum, including four years of pre-professional study in college (premed), four years of medical school, and three to four years of graduate medical education in a teaching hospital (internship and residency). The students in medical school are referred to as "undergraduate" medical students, even though they are college graduates. Residency training is referred to as "graduate" medical education. Beyond this formal training, the physician is expected to pursue lifelong learning through continuing education.

Medical education as it exists today is vastly different from early medical training. During the early colonization of America, it was relatively simple: Students learned from a practitioner who, as preceptor, taught them skills and knowledge. By the time of the American Revolution, the shortcomings of preceptorships were becoming recognized, and the idea of the medical school was introduced. Most nineteenth century medical schools, however, were proprietary institutions, not nonprofit colleges. Courses were didactic, intended to supplement but not offer clinical teaching. Generally, they had low standards of teaching and poor facilities, and they admitted any student who could pay the required tuition. The proprietary schools, because they competed with each other as well as schools affiliated with universities, even attempted to make their programs more attractive by offering free trips to Europe upon graduation to those students who paid fees regularly and in cash for three years (Stevens 1971). Therefore, anyone who could afford it could obtain a medical degree and practice medicine.

In 1904, the American Medical Association established the Council on Medical Education to begin efforts to upgrade medical education and to become the AMA's agency for implementing educational change. Over time, the council became an important regulating agency in establishing high standards in medical schools and in strengthening the AMA's influence in medical education. Perhaps the most powerful event in helping the subsequent success of these efforts was the Flexner Report.

The Flexner Report of 1910 is today considered one of the most important events in the history of medical education. After visiting every medical school in the country, Abraham Flexner issued a report exposing the generally inadequate and substandard state of medical education in the United States. With the exception of only three medical schools (Harvard, Western Reserve, and Johns Hopkins) that were given full approval, most other schools were described, for example, as "utterly wretched," "out-and-out commercial enterprises," or "wholly inadequate" (Stevens 1971, p. 67).

The Flexner Report strongly recommended that medical schools employ full-time faculty and that both hospital and laboratory facilities be available to medical students. It recommended that admissions standards for students be established and that the qualifications of the medical school faculty be raised. Flexner urged that the Johns Hopkins program be used as a model of medical education—that a bachelor's degree with certain premedical courses be required for admission, that the university be responsible for graduate-level medical education, and that teaching and research be integrated within the institution.

As a result of the Flexner Report and strong public support, most of the 400 or so proprietary schools were eliminated so that by 1920, only 50 schools were accredited. Because the only source of medical school ratings continued to be the AMA's Council on Medical Education, it was able to function as an effective monopoly over the regulation of medical education.

Between 1920 and World War II, medical schools continued the long process of professional reform, continuing to follow the standards recommended by the Flexner Report. At that time, the format of two undergraduate years of basic sciences followed by two years of clinical education, still generally practiced today, was instituted.

Following World War II, the affiliation of hospital teaching programs with university medical schools became increasingly common. As a result, residency training also became increasingly available and was no longer viewed as something extra; rather, specialization was quickly becoming the rule instead of the exception. The number of certified specialists tripled between 1940 and 1951 (Dietrick and Berson 1953), and by 1980 that number had again substantially increased.

Initially, each national specialty assumed responsibility for the accreditation of its own residency program because

American medical schools did not want to become involved with specialty training. It was not until 1972 that the residency accreditation structure was finally reformed and all graduate programs across the country were governed by one committee and the policies and standards it set. This new committee, the Liaison Committee on Graduate Medical Education, was a logical and probably inevitable extension of the already existing Liaison Committee on Medical Education that had been established for undergraduate education in 1942. Thus, a continuity in medical training was finally underway.

Until the emergence of that continuity in 1972, medical education had been divided into two essentially distinct phases—the undergraduate program leading to the M.D. degree and the graduate program leading to certification in a specialty. With the modernization of medicine, however, has come a "blurring of the traditional boundaries between undergraduate and graduate medical education" (Cooper 1974, p. 49).

Goode, in his analysis of the characteristics of the profession, summarizes well the historical outcomes achieved by the medical profession:

> *The medical profession had not only met the basic criteria of being a service occupation supported by prolonged training in a specialized knowledge, but furthermore, it had determined its own standards of education and training, had successfully demanded high-caliber students, had staffed its own licensing and admission boards, had shaped legislation in its own interests, had developed stringent professional sanctions, had become a terminal occupation and was free of formal lay evaluation and control* (cited in Cockerham 1982, p. 135).

A final factor shaping the history of medical education remains to be mentioned—medical research. During World War II, the U.S. government so successfully supported technological and war-related medical research that after the war the government continued to generously finance medical research in a wide variety of areas. Private foundations and categorical disease organizations also became generous sources of funding. As a result, this emphasis on research was and still is very influential in directing the focus of medicine and its subsequent impact on medical education. For the 20 years following World War II:

The name of the game was laboratory and clinical research, and academic appointments and promotions were tied to research productivity. Teaching and patient care were necessary evils and "teaching materials," which were patients with esoteric diseases or those on whom a research project was being conducted, were the principal occupants of the wards of university hospitals (Gellhorn 1979, pp. 158–59).

The production of biomedical research publications reached spectacular proportions, contributing to a significant increase in biomedical knowledge. The effect of this era of highly financed research was that all potential medical students, to be capable of understanding and contributing to the field of biomedical knowledge, had to be of superior intellect and have a scientific background. Thus began the extremely rigorous and highly emphasized science-related background of the physician-to-be.

As the system of medical education developed over the years, students have pointed to several structural components of their educational process, running the continuum from premedical education through residency training, as "built-in sources of stress." One of the first significant sources of stress facing the would-be physician begins well before medical school, in the preparation for medical school. The overwhelming majority of medical schools require biology, inorganic and organic chemistry, physics, and mathematics with calculus. Because the grade point average (GPA) and the Medical College Aptitude Test (MCAT) are the two statistics of greatest interest to admissions committees, competition for grades is typically relentless.

Serious college students often bypass, when possible, required courses for premedical students because they wish to avoid the disparate competitiveness and preoccupation with grades which sourly colour learning. Many young men and women who enter college with the aspiration to enter medicine are so distressed by the

*obsession of their premedical contemporaries with
grades that they abandon their career plan* (Gellhorn
1979, p. 160).

Over the years it has become common knowledge that
cheating and perhaps even sabotage occur on a large scale
as students strive to attain a GPA high enough to impress
admissions committees. A common complaint among
students is that medical schools and colleges disagree too
much on what is required of a medical student. Many
students feel ill advised and note that if they could do it
over again, they would take more courses in the humani-
ties because they feel the need for a broader background
(Sierles, Hendrick, and Circle 1980).

The typical format imposed upon medical students is
two years of basic sciences followed by two years of clinical
study. Basic science courses are taught almost exclusively
in the classroom; they are a great source of disappointment
and stress to many medical students. Most students have
just completed four years of highly competitive hard science in premedical education, only to graduate back to the
status of undergraduate. Their idealized expectations of
helping people, treating patients, and fighting disease are
met with longer classroom hours, even more complex
scientific learning, continued competition, and little if any
contact with patients. Disillusionment is common, and
students complain overwhelmingly that too much learning is forced and that much of it seems irrelevant to patient care.

Built-in sources of stress also occur for those in residency programs. A more or less unspoken assumption has
evolved that "everyone in medical school goes into a
specialty field." In the past, only a small percentage of
those graduating from medical school went on to specialize
in graduate training programs, but today over 90 percent of
those graduating from medical school specialize. This
pressure is difficult to ignore.

Along with the pressure to specialize comes the stress of
competition for acceptance into a residency program,
including not only the field of one's choice but also the
medical school of one's choice. Competition does not end,
however, with one's acceptance into a residency program.
Rather, it intensifies. The title of chief resident during the

third or fourth year, for example, carries status for which competition takes place during the first two years. Those interested in pursuing fellowships after residency must compete to demonstrate competence in those qualities that are sought in academic medicine. And some programs in medicine today still adhere to a pyramid system—a residency program that can graduate only five students at the end of three years but that nevertheless accepts 10 students in the first year. Weeding out the extra five students unnecessarily pushes stress to its extreme.

The element of age is yet another potential cause of stress that is built into the structure of graduate medical education. At the minimum, if students have never (since the first grade) taken a break in their education, they will be at least 26 years old when applying to a residency training program. While the vast majority of their contemporaries will already have graduated and achieved some degree of financial and social independence, physicians-to-be are still competing for schools and out of necessity still financially and socially dependent. For many, this prolonged state of competition and dependence requires a wealth of coping skills that may not necessarily be available.

Two additional sources of stress common to both pre-medical and medical education are a result of recent changes in the economic structure of the United States. First, available financial support is continually dwindling as government loans and stipends are cut back substantially or cut out all together. In fact, government loans or stipends for graduate medical students are essentially nonexistent. The competition for scholarships has of course become ferociously competitive, leaving most students in the 1980s to create their own program of financial support. According to the American Association of Medical Colleges (AAMC), the average indebtedness upon graduation of a medical student today ranges from $35,000 to $50,000, with payback typically beginning within six months of graduation from residency.

The situation of indebtedness then leads to the second problem—the maldistribution of physicians. Newly graduated physicians hesitate to practice in a small community where their earning power may not be as great or as consistent as in an urban environment. It is understandable that for most graduates, the ability to at last afford some long-awaited possessions for self and family—as well as to make loan payments—takes on some priority. Additionally, most graduates prefer to build a new practice in a larger city or near a medical center where the facilities and consultations to which they are accustomed are readily available. The Graduate Medical Education National Advisory Committee warns, however, that a significant oversupply of physicians in many urban areas and in certain specialties is likely by 1990. This possibility represents one more concern that medical students and residents must consider in their choice of medical specialty.

Today's medical students are expected to be the cream of the nation's crop. Inherent within any such extensive and highly structured system is the built-in potential for stress.

Sources of Stress—Medical Students

A longitudinal study of a sample of Harvard students (Vaillant 1977) demonstrated that "potentially stressful events may generate incapacitating responses or trigger adaptive mechanisms that eventually lead to renewed strength" (Mumford 1983, p. 436). Whether stressful events "generate incapacitating responses" or "trigger adaptive mechanisms" speaks to the complex interaction between the demands of medical school and the coping mechanisms available to students. The four-year medical curriculum can be conceptualized as presenting the student with a series of adaptive and developmental tasks (Bojar 1971; Gaensbauer and Mizner 1980; Lief et al. 1960; Pfeiffer 1983). An article written by Gaensbauer and Mizner (1980) is particularly helpful in this conceptualization. It hypothesizes that students' emotional problems derive as much from the nature of the developmental stresses they must face as from their own individual vulnerability and that to study these developmental stresses might prove fruitful in determining what types of coping strategies or tasks would be most helpful. To do so, Gaensbauer and Mizner reviewed the files of all students who had sought psychiatric consultation at the University of Colorado Medical School over the preceding 10 years. They then categorized the timing and the nature of the consultations.

From that information, they attempted to "identify recurring themes which might reflect specific developmental issues which must be dealt with by all medical students" (p. 61). The following discussion of stress among medical students uses Gaensbauer and Mizner's work as a point of departure and identifies the specific developmental tasks that confront students and the ensuing stresses likely to occur when they are not successfully managed.

First year

During the first year of medical school, academic pressures rank as the greatest source of stress in students' lives (Boyle and Coombs 1971). Academic pressures include the complexity of the material to be learned and the competition; students no longer stand out as academically superior because nearly everyone in their class is academically superior. Fear of failure may arise for perhaps the first time in a student's life. Therefore, an initial task for the first-year student is to determine personal capabilities in this new context and to perform in a manner that equals one's ability, while maintaining a sense of adequacy. Failure to develop such coping strategies is likely to result in decreased self-esteem, depression, and anxiety. Common results of the unsuccessful resolution of these tasks are withdrawal from competition and inability to perform at one's best level.

During the first of medical school, academic pressures rank as the greatest source of [student] stress.

A freshman medical student was seen approximately two months after the beginning of school because of severe anxiety around the time of examinations and serious doubts about whether he could handle the academic stresses of medical school. He described long-standing problems of low self-esteem, particularly in comparison with his father and older sister, who had had brilliant academic careers. His choice of medicine had been an attempt to stake out an area of excellence for himself by combining his scientific interests with his ability to relate humanistically to others. The competitive, heavily scientific orientation of the first two years had thrown him into the high pressure academic situation in which he felt most ill at ease, and he became increasingly anxious and depressed. Reassurance and the opportunity to ventilate his concerns were sufficient to significantly allay his doubts (Gaensbauer and Mizner 1980, p. 61).

Another major source of stress for freshmen medical students is the vast quantity of material to be learned—so vast in fact that there is no way to learn it at all. The task therefore becomes one of setting self-imposed limits on the amount of material to be learned. For many medical students, who by nature have an "obsessive-compulsive" make-up, the feeling of less than complete mastery is very difficult to accept. For those who cannot accept this tolerance for some uncertainty in their learning, the result is often extreme anxiety and the feeling of being "driven" to the extent that psychological intervention is required.

In addition to academic demands, a third major stress (actually a result of the first two) is apparent—the lack of time for personal and social relationships. Social relationships at this time are typically disrupted as friends from college move on and entrance into medical school often means a move away from home. Given the immense demands on one's time, the task of reestablishing and building new social relationships may prove very difficult. The student has a growing sense of the sacrifices that a career in medicine will require, and even though adaptation to such sacrifices will be required throughout medical school and residency, the potential for maladaptive coping is particularly great in the first year. A common mistake of first-year medical students (a maladaptive coping strategy) is to make academics a higher priority than personal and emotional needs. The resulting risk is one of loneliness and alienation from supportive relationships, including marital partners. Another maladaptive coping strategy is to seek situations that will meet the student's need for dependency but demand little in return—for example, moving back home with parents who will provide financial and emotional support or selecting a readily available spouse who will do the same. To the extent that such choices represent a kind of psychosocial regression, the long-term outcome is not apt to be positive even though in the short run such a choice does appear workable.

A final source of stress for freshmen students evolves from the discrepancy between their lofty expectations of medical school and what medical school turns out to be. For students:

the mystique of the medical school is strong, and from the beginning there are disappointments—poor lectures, inadequate material, repetitive material, fragmentation of subjects, and a lack of coordination. It only helped a little to recognize an exaggerated high level of aspiration, which intensifies disappointment (Rosenberg 1971, p. 213).

In trying to summarize the many and varied disappointments they had experienced, these students coined a phrase, the "double message," to describe how they felt. Faculty talked about treating patients but taught basic sciences, talked about awareness of the total situation but taught fragmented disease and symptoms, disparaged studying trivia yet called for it on examinations, and insisted on laboratory sessions yet looked the other way when students copied down the right answers because time was too short for real experimentation. Such game playing starts the process of disillusionment early for many medical students.

Second year
The major stresses in the second year appear to highlight the issue of commitment for many medical students. Fatigue is increased (longer hours in the classroom and continued pressure to perform on examinations) and still there is little or no actual patient contact. Students therefore find themselves needing to determine how much they want to be doctors. They must decide whether they can make the commitment to work as long and as hard as they must with few immediate rewards. Students able to come to terms with this issue will likely learn to persevere and tolerate hard work. Students unable to come to terms with the issue are likely to have feelings of doubt or resentment that will continue to affect both current and future performance, including patient care.

A second major stress of the second year is the exposure to clinical problems in pathology, pharmacology, and psychiatry. The impact of these courses on students can produce considerable anxiety and hypochondriasis (abnormal anxiety over one's health, often with imagined illnesses). For medical students, hypochondriasis has an added twist: Students think they have or may get whatever disease they are studying. This occurrence is common enough that it is lightheartedly referred to as "medical students' disease." The phenomenon is not to be taken lightly, however (Bojar 1971; Hunter, Lohrenz, and Schwartzman 1964; Saslow 1956; Woods, Natterson, and Silverson 1966). Thus, another major task arises for the second-year medical student—to develop a sense of detachment about the study of disease and illness without losing sight of its human implications. Inability to achieve this task can result in preoccupation with one's health and severe stress, which in turn interfere with the student's ability to learn important material.

> *A second-year student was referred because of abdominal and chest pains which were felt to be musculoskeletal and tension related. A mild elevation of blood pressure had been found during a recent physical examination. There was a strong family history of cardiovascular disease on both sides. A maternal uncle had died suddenly of a heart attack several months earlier. On his father's side, his grandfather and an uncle had died of cardiovascular causes. Studying pathology stimulated his thinking about all the possible diseases he might have. Lectures on the cardiovascular system had been so distressing that he had stopped attending them. A short-term supportive psychotherapeutic experience enabled him to put his blood pressure findings in perspective and allowed him to return to class* (Gaensbauer and Mizner 1980, p. 64).

A third major stress during the second year carries over from the first year—lack of time for family, friends, and recreation. The result is often a feeling of dehumanization deriving from this "tunnel vision"; it occurs when students' excessive academic demands preclude time for any pursuit of personal needs or interests.

Third year
Many authors regard the third year as most important to the student's identity as a physician (Gaensbauer and

Mizner 1980). Beginning with this year, students move from the relatively impersonal learning of theory to a role in which they must apply the theory—with less structure and less regular feedback than they have had for the past six years. The question of being able to manage competently arises in students' minds.

The most intense of experiences to confront and create stress for the third year student is that of death and dying. Acceptance of death and of one's own helplessness in certain situations is a crucial task for students. Those who have difficulties coping with this stress may find that they tend to withdraw from such situations or feel unable to empathize with patients and their families or attempt overly heroic forms of treatment that fail to take into account the wishes of patients and their families. Students might also attempt to cope with this type of situation by regarding the patient as a biomedical problem rather than as a whole person with whom one might closely identify.

> *A third-year medical student had received poor evaluations on his initial clinical rotations. Problem behavior on the wards had alternated between absences from the wards at times when he was expected and the aggressive taking on of responsibilities for which he was not qualified without consultation with staff. Much of his behavior could be traced to his inability to tolerate feelings of helplessness in the face of so many sick and dying patients. His intolerance of this stress was ultimately of such severity that he was requested to withdraw from school* (Gaensbauer and Mizner 1980, p. 65).

Contact with patients, with all its emotional intensity, and everyday less interesting problems can provoke a crisis related to issues of intimacy and closeness. Therefore, students must learn to develop a tolerance for emotionally intense situations yet maintain an empathetic involvement with patients.

Along with learning to interact with patients in a clinical setting comes learning to interact with other medical staff, often in pressured situations. Medical students begin to sense a familiar pattern occurring in their education process—continually graduating to a new "undergraduate" role (from college, to the first two years of medical school, and now to the clinical setting). Students must be able to tolerate being told what to do and to have their mistakes continually pointed out without becoming unreasonably anxious, angry, or depressed. A common stress reaction is performance anxiety, especially during oral presentations and when learning clinical procedures. Learning to tolerate receiving orders, having one's errors delineated, and being the low person in the hierarchy of ward personnel (where nurses have more practical knowledge than do students) is a major task. Failure to do so will likely result in overt anxiety whenever in the clinical setting, argumentativeness and hostility (both coming from and directed to the student), and lowered self-esteem from the inability to make a significant contribution to the health team.

Lack of time for family, friends, and recreation continues to be a major concern for third-year students (some rank it first) (Edwards and Zimet 1976). Medical students are therefore still experiencing the feelings of dehumanization and disillusionment that accompany this major stressor, which at this point may well fit into the category of chronic stress.

Fourth year

The fourth year is usually less stressful for students than the previous three years. Clinical work is essentially similar to the third year, and students have more time for electives in areas where their interests are greatest. Requests for therapy by fourth-year students are typically fewer (Gaensbauer and Mizner 1980; Hunter, Prince, and Schwartzman 1961; Pfeiffer 1983). The events that provoke the most stress at this time reflect concerns about graduation and the ability to perform responsibly as "real" physicians.

A fourth-year student expressed concern about his adequacy as a clinician, including concern that he had a memory disturbance which interfered with his ability to remember clinical material. He had recently returned to a clinical rotation after eight months of nonclinical electives, and also had had to make a decision about application for internships the previous week. He had decided to apply for an internship in a subspecialty which he perceived as a quite circumscribed field, the

*major reason being "I think I can handle it." Doubts
about his clinical competence and memory had persisted
despite the fact that he had never failed a course, nor
had his qualifications for being a physician ever been
called into question by instructors. In a brief psychotherapy, drawing attention to the immediate precipitants
of his seeking help, and to his overly critical self-
assessment was sufficient to relieve much of his anxiety*
(Gaensbauer and Mizner 1980, p. 66).

Additional sources of stress at this time center around
the prospect of ending a phase in one's life and moving on,
a type of loss for some students. Competition for residency
positions and indecision over choice of specialty are also
prominent (Adsett 1968). And fourth-year students find the
amount of noneducational service they are required to
perform a major source of stress.

The lack of time for family and friends continues to be a
major concern (Edwards and Zimet 1976). This source of
stress speaks to the need to develop coping strategies that
will assist in striking a proper balance between one's personal and professional life (Hunter, Lohrenz, and Schwartzman 1964). Compromise is necessary but to some extent
likely to be painful because time spent in either professional or personal activities will detract from the other.
The attempt to make these compromises as satisfactory
as possible is an ongoing challenge.

It appears that medical students, despite the long hours
of study, competition, and social isolation that begin early
in the preparation for medical school, "enter medical
school openly idealistic about the practice of medicine and
the medical profession and feel that medicine is the best of
all professions, but that during the course of medical
school students develop a cynical attitude toward the daily
routine of medical school" (Becker et al. 1961). A more
recent study confirms this statement, describing medical
school as "the process of disillusionment" (Schwarz et
al. 1978).

Solutions—Medical Students
The concept of stress inoculation (Meichenbaum 1977)
suggests that to provide students with information, feedback, and choices would be to offer great protection from
the disruptive and demoralizing effects associated with

decisions that have a high potential for negative consequences. Perhaps then solutions involving this concept could prove useful in bringing to a halt or at least minimizing the "process of disillusionment" so prevalent among medical students.

A crucial place to begin is before medical students ever begin medical school, that is, during premedical education (Funkenstein 1968; Gottheil et al. 1969; Huebner, Royer, and Moore 1981). Many students have only vague notions of what it means to be a physician in today's world. To them the physician is the old-fashioned stereotype—the kind, fatherly gentleman who uses his vast supply of knowledge to cure his patients. To avert the problems that arise when the actual situation is found to be substantially different from this romanticized notion, students need more information about what the life of a physician is really like. One solution is to provide students with first-hand experience by having access to older and respected individuals to whom they could go for advice or to follow during a typical day in the office or hospital (Funkenstein 1968).

A second solution is to provide students with information *and* the potential for more control, that is, a formalized orientation for all incoming freshmen. A recently revised orientation program at the University of Missouri–Columbia School of Medicine includes the essential ingredients for successful orientation:

> *The new program was less formal, less intimidating, more supportive, and more personal; the program included counseling about potential stressors, expectations, time management, evaluation, and grading (including the dean's letter). Spouses and children participated in various orientation events. A student handbook was drafted to provide follow-up information about governance, administration, health care, counseling, evaluation and grading, clerkships, and specialty choice. A series of class meetings and workshops during years 2 and 3 introduced students to a strategy of sequencing clerkships and of preparing for decision making regarding specialty areas and specific residency program choices* (Huebner, Royer, and Moore 1981, p. 557).

Such an extensive and practical orientation should help those students with unrealistic expectations to adjust them to a more realistic level, thereby preventing the greater dissatisfaction with medical school that occurs when expectations and realities are mismatched (Gottheil et al. 1969).

A third solution, in response to consistent complaints from students, is to clarify the curriculum and professors' evaluations of students. The issues of information, feedback, and choices are again applicable. Students rightly expect clear course objectives and criteria for evaluation and feedback as quickly as possible on examinations. Clarifying the curriculum also includes the workload expected. Professors should be selective in the topics they decide to cover. The challenge offered to the student must be great enough to facilitate optimal learning but not so great as to inhibit learning (the Yerkes-Dobson law discussed earlier).

A professor's ability to successfully plan the curriculum and provide timely evaluation is often a reflection of the ability to be a good teacher. Thus, a fourth solution is apparent: Teaching must be professionalized and given the same prestige as other faculty activities. Because the emphasis in most medical schools is on research and consultation, the quality of teaching has not improved. Most faculty have never been taught any pedagogical techniques; rather they are expected to perpetuate the myth that excellence in research makes for excellence in teaching. Until merit in teaching like merit in research is rewarded, this situation is unlikely to change.

The lack of time for family, friends, and recreation results for many students in feelings of dehumanization, depression, and dependency and in passive, mechanized coping styles that eliminate emotions and feelings in the name of better survival. A suggested solution for preventing these results involves increasing the flexibility of the medical school curriculum (Pfeiffer 1983). Alternative curricular tracks might be offered that would allow for the option of completing medical school over a longer period of time. Not only would a more prolonged and less intense setting increase students' comfort with learning vast amounts of material; it would also allow more time for achieving those necessary developmental tasks of independence, intimacy, and self-actualization. More flexibility would also allow for more part-time work, which would result in increased financial independence. And all students would benefit from definite breaks and vacation time when they can relax away from the stress of medicine. A flexible curriculum offers perhaps the most opportunity for students to assume more control over their lives, because the choices really are accessible and attainable.

Another solution is to reevaluate the grading system. "Does the bell-shaped grading system with all the anxiety it engenders really describe the ability of such a highly selected group of students?" (Pfeiffer 1983, p. 133). What of those few students who receive lower grades? Because the differences are so minor, how important are they? Schools that must continue this traditional grading format should be especially supportive of the students whose scores fall toward the lower end of the curve.

The final suggested solution is to appoint a medical school ombudsman. A new program currently underway at Stanford University Medical Center illustrates this solution (Weinstein 1983). In response to the charge that the medical school environment helps to train and develop maladaptive patterns in their students, the associate dean of student affairs established the Committee on the Well-Being of Medical Students and House Staff. The task of this group was to assess the problems and needs of both populations. It was comprised of students from each year selected by the medical students' organization, three house officers who volunteered out of their own interests, and several academic and clinical faculty who were selected by the associate dean because they had shown interest in student affairs in the past. A survey assessed those areas perceived as problematic for students and their partners, and the committee generated proposals to alleviate the problems. The medical school ombudsman, appointed as the result of one of the committee's proposals, has been shown to be consistently beneficial. Students have been able to channel their grievances and to effect change, typically around issues of academics, teaching quality, student-teacher relationships, and student services. "Some distress can be relieved by such simple techniques as providing information and appointing individuals as advocates with clearly defined roles in relation to those in training" (Weinstein 1983, p. 380).

One of the most crucial roles to be fulfilled by an ombudsman is that of developing and sanctioning mechanisms enabling students to seek professional help without stigma. Students without this mechanism are usually unwilling to seek assistance from colleagues, instructors, or therapists within the medical school for fear that it may be a sign of weakness that will affect their reputation and record. Indeed, in many schools the same person who writes letters of recommendation and promotion simultaneously acts as student counselor or therapist. An obvious conflict of interest is at play in this situation; students become so concerned about confidentiality that they will unlikely approach this person, choosing instead to continue under unrelieved stress with increased feelings of helplessness. In a recent survey of 114 medical schools, counseling services were available but underused as a result of poor communication about their availability and concern about confidentiality (Seigle, Schuckit, and Plumb 1983). The following model counseling program could help increase the use of currently available services:

1. *Group seminars should be organized to discuss emotional conflicts in medicine and effective coping. Information about personal counseling could be provided or referrals could be made directly from the group. Confidentiality should be guaranteed and emphasized.*
2. *Quarterly announcements or bulletins about counseling should provide access to information when students are most receptive.*
3. *Counseling should be separated from the student affairs office so that it would not be construed as overlapping with administrative responsibilities such as evaluations.*
4. *Faculty members should be encouraged and trained to recognize stress among students and refer them to the appropriate contacts.*
5. *Formalized referral to psychiatrists in the community should be made through the student health service or a qualified person outside of the dean's office.*

> *6. Personal counseling should be strictly confidential with repeated assurances. Seeking or receiving counseling should never be used for promotion or dismissal* (Seigle, Schuckit, and Plumb 1983, p. 545).

The medical profession should be able to serve as a model in the recognition, referral, and treatment of stress in medical students so that they as physicians will be better trained to deal with their own stress and the stress of their patients as well.

In all cases, each of these suggested solutions to help reduce and prevent distress among students is implemented primarily by the medical school system itself. While students' impact and support is inherent throughout, cooperation from the medical school is required. Another approach is to implement solutions entirely independent of the medical school system. These solutions address the issue of what medical students can do to help themselves.

One of the most useful and well-documented solutions generated primarily by students is the development of student support groups (Gaensbauer and Mizner 1980; Huebner, Royer, and Moore 1981; Pfeiffer 1983; Siegel and Donnelly 1978; Webster and Robinowitz 1979; Weinstein 1983). Although receptive medical school faculty facilitate the establishment of student groups, curriculum committees do not formally acknowledge them, nor is credit given. Students typically initiate the organization of a group by demonstrating interest or need to trusted faculty and then as a group determine content, time, and duration for the particular group. Content for support groups varies widely, but for all the purposes are the same: to obtain support and to get some relief from the stresses of medical education. Some read nonmedical literature, others seek to get information on residency programs and specialties, others form study groups and tutorials, others meet with their spouses. Members of the groups share frustrations about school and their personal lives, establish close friendships with peers and faculty, and learn stress- and time-management techniques.

> *Belonging to and being accepted as a member of the group was a very important factor for me personally. I found it very helpful to be in a setting where we could*

all, to some degree, shed the facade of cool self-assurance that we were encouraged to build for ourselves during our "in-hospital" lives, and share more of ourselves (Webster and Robinowitz 1979, p. 60).

Another solution to reduce stress is living arrangements (Huebner, Royer, and Moore 1981). Stress appears to be less for those living with a spouse or cohabitant and greatest for those living alone. Even though time spent with a significant other is time taken away from studying, the mediating effects on stress of interpersonal relationships and psychological support systems is an important payoff.

Stress appears to be less for those living with a spouse or cohabitant and greatest for those living alone.

A final self-help solution suggested to medical students is to seek out a faculty member with whom a long-term relationship can be developed. For many, this cultivation of a mentor has proved useful in gaining a role model, academic advice, and a trusted friend within the system who can offer support and counsel from first-hand experience.

It is commonly accepted that medical education is a time of stress. Students develop strategies for and styles of coping with this stress to survive, typically at the expense of those nearest to them, including themselves. It is ironic that in the training of a profession for which compassion, warmth, and caring are considered essential ingredients in the care of patients, individuals in training must undergo so many personal deprivations. Perhaps the greatest concern is that students will adhere to those short-term, survival-oriented styles of coping when they become practicing physicians. The development of a greater repertoire of coping mechanisms should result in confining stress to moderate levels, where learning ability is optimal.

Sources of Stress—Medical Residents

If the first years of medical school are a "process of disillusionment," what then might the next three to five years of residency be called? The stresses of residency training are at least as significant as those of medical school (Weinstein 1983); many authors assert that residency training is more stressful than medical school, especially the first year, known as the internship (Cousins 1981; Miller 1981; Siegel and Donnelly 1978; Valko and Clayton 1975).

I have been able to meet with medical students and physicians at various stages in their training and their careers. The weakest link in the entire chain of physician training, it seems to me, is the ordeal known as the internship. More specifically, I refer to the theory that it is necessary to put medical school graduates through a human meat grinder before they can qualify as full-fledged physicians (Cousins 1981, p. 377).

The internship year is "a time of insecurity and lack of confidence, of frustration and anxiety, of anomie and disillusionment (Bates, Hinton, and Wood 1973, p. 611). And the American Medical Association has labeled first-year residents as a group "at risk" for becoming impaired (Tokarz, Bremer, and Peters 1979). What is it about the nature of the internship year that jeopardizes the physical and emotional health of those immersed in it?

Internship/first-year residency

One of the first sources of stress an intern encounters is the actual geographical move to a new state and city and a new medical school, and the unfamiliar housing, shopping, transportation, and social networks he or she encounters. Lack of a formalized, friendly, and useful orientation for interns and their spouses is a common complaint and an ongoing source of stress because individuals must make their own way in this new environment. Many unmarried interns have no immediately available sources of social support to help make the transition less stressful. This transition from medical school to residency is often compared to the transition from premedical school to medical school. The sources of stress involved in the change are similar, as is the inability or unwillingness of the medical school system to make the transition less stressful.

The internship year is a critical period for young physicians and their ability to learn successful coping strategies. It is clearly an important bridge between student and full-fledged professional and thus a time of role change. The implications of this role change are varied, and each is a potential source of stress. First, interns must simultaneously become primary care providers and teachers of medical students while once again finding themselves at the bottom of the training and hospital hierarchy. This situation often translates into little emotional or physical support in one's work. The goal of an intern therefore often becomes one of mere survival. Perhaps the one factor most consistently cited as a major source of stress is lack of sleep, the result of a workload greater than 100 hours per week (Asken and Raham 1983; Friedman, Bigger, and Kornfeld 1971; Friedman, Kornfeld, and Bigger 1973; Valko and Clayton 1975). Over one-third of the house staff members in one study felt that their efficiency was significantly compromised because of overwork (Wilkinson, Tyler, and Varey 1975). Reactions by sleep-deprived interns include a significant increase in errors, difficulty in thinking, sensitivity to criticism, depersonalization, an inappropriate affect and black humor, and deficits in recent memory (Friedman, Kornfeld, and Bigger 1973). Long hours cause irritability and declining abilities to deal with family and interpersonal relations (Wilkinson, Tyler, and Varey 1975). It appears probable that interns' ability to cope successfully (to balance the degree of stress encountered and the coping strategies available) may well be affected most by the night call schedule and the related loss of sleep—especially when one considers that the most frequently used coping strategy for sleep-deprived interns is to spend all their free time sleeping.

The internship may have an equally important effect on the intern's personal development as well. Coping mechanisms the intern relies upon to deal with the stresses of this year may well be a key factor in future personal and professional development and well-being. Continually using strategies during internship that encourage emotional detachment in dealing with patients and family (strategies typically learned and developed during medical school) may result in the development of habitually avoiding feelings. This detached concern is then likely to permeate both personal and professional life.

It makes me a dull and uninteresting person. When I get home after a night on call, if it's been a busy night, I'm sort of a blob. I want to be fed, I want to take a shower and I want to go to bed. Creature comforts are uppermost in my life usually. It takes a real effort and sometimes some coaxing by my wife to get me to come out of my shell and relate to her. Fatigue dulls your sensitivi-

ties and your ability to relate to other people and to enjoy life. It makes you irritable, angry, more susceptible to being ticked off by minor inconveniences. You're more likely to be an unattractive person to relate to. . . .

The lack of sleep and the ridiculous hours are outrageous. There's no reason for it, it's an economic reason, an initiation rite. Maybe there's something to say for dealing with stress over those long hours of time that makes you a better person, but you don't learn more, there's a point of diminishing returns in delivering care. I just think that's outrageous (Callan 1983, pp. 59, 62).

Second- and third-year residents

Second- and third-year residents are also subject to a variety of stressors, some that are merely continuations and others that are specific to the last years of residency training. Continued stressors include the lack of free time for leisure, recreation, and family, and financial problems and responsibilities. Just as the medical school environment presented a great many stresses and pressures that greatly impeded the attainment of an adult identity part of and apart from the professional role and the formation of long-term intimate relationships, so does residency. Issues of independence also arise for residents because of the prolonged state of dependency that medical education has imposed upon them. The inability to move successfully through these developmental tasks often results in isolation and depression (Valko and Clayton 1975), marital problems (Bates and Carroll 1975), emotional instability (Tokarz, Bremer, and Peters 1979), and disillusionment about medicine (Bates, Hinton, and Wood 1973).

Major stressors specific to the latter part of residency are a separation crisis and studying for the medical board examination.

Every year shortly after New Year, the third year resident tends to experience unusually emphatic feelings of turmoil and stress. During this time there typically will be more arguments with staff, more tardiness, delinquency, sloppier record keeping, and louder complaining and back-biting. The intensity and yearly regularity of this phenomenon suggest that each class of graduating

residents experiences a form of separation crisis (Merkel
and Walbroehl 1980, p. 366).

This phenomenon is not unlike adolescents' acting out
their separation crises when their time for departure from
family occurs. Residents, because of their prolonged dependency, are like adolescents; at graduation they must
depart with their newly acquired adult identity as physicians. Studying for the medical board examination at this
same time increases both stress and fatigue. A typical
method of coping to make the separation easier is therefore
to find fault with everything and everybody. This fault-
finding justifies the need and desirability to leave in the
minds of residents. Unfortunately, other staff and younger
residents are too often unaware that such a crisis exists;
they react in an equally disagreeable, offended, and angry
manner. The rate and quality of learning are compromised
when this negative state is allowed to continue.

Solutions—Medical Residents
Recommendations to prevent and reduce stress for medical
residents are similar to those for undergraduate medical
students, and they too fall into the categories of help from
the medical school structure and self-help.

The first suggestion, like that for undergraduate medical
students, is to provide a formalized orientation for all new
residents and their spouses. Typically, new interns are
from another state and/or another part of the country.
Information about such mundane matters as evening
meals, bus service to outlying hospitals, reasonably priced
housing, and low-cost counseling services for residents and
their spouses can make the lives of residents easier; such a
program has in fact been implemented in a pilot project at
the Stanford Medical School (Weinstein 1983). In addition,
clearly stated requirements for patient care, learning, and
teaching should result in more mutual than discrepant
expectations among residents and faculty.

Another obvious but surprisingly neglected solution is to
redesign the work schedule. To provide an intern with
fewer continuous working hours and therefore more sleep
and more personal time is reasonable (Callan 1983). Flexible-
time residencies have also been suggested (Howell 1974;

Shapiro and Driscoll 1979). Probably not widely understood is the requirement that all residency programs offer flexible-time residencies; unspoken expectations, however, usually prevent their use by other than a few—usually women with young children or pregnant women close to delivery. Perhaps the reason such scheduling is not more widely used is that even though flexible-time schedules enable two people to share one position and earn half the salary, each still works two-thirds of the time—or over 60 hours per week!

Residents, unlike medical students, do not receive regular feedback to know whether they are meeting requirements and satisfying expectations. Therefore, providing consistent feedback through formalized channels would help alleviate the stress provoked by uncertainty. Feedback should include praise for work well done as well as clarification of areas needing further work. It is necessary not only to provide assistance in effecting change but also to provide it early in the year so that the resident has adequate time in which to make the change.

To assist residents in dealing with the stresses surrounding separation crises, residency programs would do well to sponsor retreats and workshops on coping with various aspects of a medical career. Practical application of the theory that information increases one's perception of control, which in turn reduces stress, might ease the transition from resident to independent practice by focusing retreats and workshops on subjects such as office- and time-management skills. Allowing third-year residents more privileges, less on-call duty, and the title of "on-call senior staff" can reinforce their beliefs in their own readiness to separate (Miller 1981).

A final solution that can be implemented by residents as well as the medical school system is the establishment of support groups for residents and their spouses. Support groups encourage reflection and provide and strengthen interpersonal support. They help to short-circuit a false assumption that is learned early during internship, that is, the implicit expectation that this is the way medicine works and that this is how the life of a physician must be. Members of a support group have the opportunity to acquire greater ability to deal with personal issues in a professional setting, a sense of decreased competitiveness with fellow residents and staff, and the exploration of alternative coping mechanisms (Siegel and Donnelly 1978).

One group of interns, whose coping styles were comprised of both active and regulating strategies (Lazarus 1966), were more likely to be rated as high performers than those whose coping style relied on only one or the other (Brent 1981). A greater coping repertoire makes possible a wider range of responses to stress, higher satisfaction, and, when combined with a high level of ego development, high performance as well.

Overall, an educational experience in medicine should be able to demonstrate that it can live up to its own dictum—"above all do no harm." Unfortunately, the reality may be otherwise. The solutions that have been offered can help educators and students reduce the stress that may result in harm and thus compromise health and learning. Increased information, feedback, and choices are the essential ingredients that make successful stress management and thus optimal learning and well-being likely.

CONCLUDING RECOMMENDATIONS

Stress is admittedly a necessary ingredient in challenging students to learn. Yet the overwhelmingly negative forms of stress that generally serve to threaten and discourage learning rather than to provide challenge and hope need to be reduced.

Universities represent a large part of the environmental force that influences stress in students. The stress-coping complex described in the first chapter outlines three points (stressors, reactive coping, active coping) where the university community can make positive interventions. Although each of the previous chapters offered specific solutions for various student groups, the monograph concludes by suggesting institutional efforts to help most students maintain a sense of control over their lives at each point on the stress-coping complex. The issue of control and its importance in reducing stress is a guiding principle in these suggestions.

The chapter presents numerous ideas to help reduce distress in students. Some of the ideas suggested are being used at many universities. The reader is cautioned, however, to evaluate the effectiveness of the programs used to implement these ideas rather than merely accept them as helpful or necessary.

A major concern is that any rehabilitation of educational programs will cost more money at a time when many educational programs are currently faced with dramatically shrinking budgets. Most of the suggestions throughout this monograph, if implemented, would cost little. Decreasing budgets, however, are certain ultimately to adversely affect the quality of teaching and thus result in the increase of stress among students.

Stressors

What constitutes a stressor and one's reactions to it often differ from individual to individual. This difference is partly the result of individuals' having varying emotional, social, and cognitive resources to cope with stress and varying psychosocial histories around stressful events. The following prescriptions to reduce distress associated with higher education are therefore oriented toward prevention of a wide variety of harmful stress reactions that can occur among students. The principles of control discussed earlier in the monograph and the closely related issues of information, feedback, and choice are inherent parts of the suggestions given. The suggestions specifically cover both students' orientation and helping students feel more control over issues related to curriculum.

Students need to become familiar with the services and activities (transportation, housing, on- or off-campus recreation, health services, counseling services, financial services, day care facilities, to name a few) within the university and the local community. Because the needs of individual students vary, many ways of informing them are possible—pamphlets, handouts, meetings, and/or social events. The point of orienting students to services and activities is ultimately to help them feel at home in their environment. This portion of the orientation would likely best be accomplished within each academic discipline—for example, graduate, law, and medical programs. Undergraduates ought to be provided this type of orientation in a group setting that is small enough for students to feel comfortable asking questions.

The point of orienting students to services and activities is . . . to help them feel at home in their environment.

An orientation for parents, spouses, and any significant others should be provided to help them anticipate students' needs and the anticipated stresses associated with being closely involved with a student. Spouses of more senior students could discuss how they "survived" and how they were able to effectively give and receive support. Spouses of senior students could share a survival list of general dos and don'ts with new students.

A number of formal and informal methods of orientation could help students better understand the academic requirements and pressures of their education. Informally, students become academically oriented through contact with their peers and more advanced students. Informal discussions with advanced students about which class to take from whom and how to do well in a particular course help at least make an unfamiliar setting more familiar; such contacts can thus help reduce stress in students (Stevens 1973). Informal contacts with faculty (for example, student/faculty parties and socials) can also benefit students and likely help them feel more hopeful about their future academic endeavors (Stevens 1973).

A number of more formal approaches are possible:

- scheduled meetings for senior students to orient new students to specific academic programs and faculty
- a student "buddy" system in which a senior student helps orient a specific new student
- meetings between faculty in each academic discipline and students to discuss how to succeed in the various programs, typical roadblocks for students, and common responses to stress
- an orientation meeting at the end of one of the first classes of the semester between the faculty member and students who are new to the school or the academic discipline
- a focus, during orientation sessions, on the challenges, consequences of mastery, hope, students' needs, and faculty members' availability to students rather than on the threatening aspects that often foster an inordinate fear of failure
- information from faculty about how students can best learn from them (for example, by memorizing content, solving problems, analyzing problems without necessarily finding solutions, integrating concepts into the larger theoretical framework, discovering the answers to questions, problems, and issues). Students can be unnecessarily confused when they do not understand that the method of learning they are accustomed to does not apply in some courses or academic disciplines.

Faculty can be particularly helpful in reducing stress by merely explaining that anxiety and self-doubt are ubiquitous among students. The stress of being a student is aggravated when one believes that he is alone with such feelings.

Another way to help reduce unnecessary stress is to give students control, information, and feedback regarding the curriculum itself. The following ways can help students deal with stress involving the curriculum:

- testing courses before they are taught
- helping students perceive themselves as successful early in their coursework

- providing alternative ways to demonstrate mastery (quizzes, exams, papers, one-on-one discussions with professors)
- providing feedback that is specific rather than general, descriptive rather than evaluative, informative rather than advice-giving, well timed, not demeaning when negative, and positive when deserved
- giving specific feedback to the class as a whole when the problems are common to many students or when many students have demonstrated mastery
- ensuring students' ongoing participation in the development of curriculum
- allowing students to evaluate course material and the teacher's performance.

In one graduate course on behavior modification of children, the professor used types of reinforcement for graduate students' performance similar to those he recommended be used for children. Interestingly enough, the graduate students in this course regularly commented on how effective such frequent and seemingly childlike reinforcement was in increasing their own interest and effort in mastering the course material. One is often left wondering why positive feedback to students is not more commonly used when it likely can have an advantageous effect on both students' learning and the reduction of stress.

Reactive Coping
The thoughts and feelings evoked by students when they are faced with a stressful event vary as much as how each chooses to cope with his own reaction to a stressor. Without the universities' directly providing any help for students feeling stressed, students will find their own effective or ineffective ways to cope. Some will choose to talk with a friend or family member; others will work their frustrations out in a gymnasium or use other forms of recreation. Others will choose alcohol, drugs, excessive eating, or other forms of self-defeating behavior. Other than providing recreational services for students, universities could make a number of services available to help students with their reactions to stressors. Many of these services would be particularly helpful to the student who is feeling helpless or who has not developed a network of support or

ways of effectively coping with the stress of school. The following forms of peer counseling have proved effective:

- telephone counseling services that provide information, crisis intervention, and referral services
- academic advice
- drug information and services
- student outreach services
- student support groups (Giddan and Austin 1982).

Faculty can also provide an important service in helping students with their reaction to stress. Faculty who have been identified as sensitive to students' needs could be used as student advocates. Student-faculty retreats (probably preferable for students beyond the undergraduate level) could help faculty and students become better acquainted and allow each to constructively air their concerns about various academic issues.

Most universities provide a student counseling center. A number of technologies used by student counseling services can help reduce stress:

- systematic desensitization
- biofeedback
- meditation
- exercise
- stress inoculation
- clarification of values
- assertiveness training
- progressive relaxation
- the combating of disabling thinking (McKay, Davis, and Fanning 1981; Mason 1980).

Active Coping
Certainly, the three points in the stress-coping complex are not mutually exclusive. Some of the points suggested to help students actively solve their own problems could also fall under ways to reduce stressors and to help students with their own reactions. Nevertheless, the following suggestions are perhaps best used as methods to help students use their own problem-solving abilities.

When individuals feel hopeful about an outcome surrounding a stressful event, they are more likely to spend their energies on active problem solving and less likely to spend them coping with their own distressful thoughts and feelings (Folkman 1982). If universities—and especially individual faculty members—want to encourage effective problem solving, they ought to consider how to instill hope in their students. For example:

- use teachers whom students evaluate positively to teach a number of the beginning courses
- reward faculty in a meaningful way both for good teaching and student advising
- provide a responsive way of handling students' complaints, including faculty members' handling their own complaints from students as well as the university's developing a formal system
- provide part-time programs to help accommodate students' personal needs
- use timely feedback so that students can correct academic problems before it is too late or realize that the professor believes they are mastering the course material
- provide information regarding various methods others use to successfully master course material.

Good teaching alone will not only help eliminate the stress associated with poor teaching but will also improve active coping as each student begins to feel that he is mastering course material. Perhaps an important way to eliminate students' distress is to ensure good teaching and to reward those who teach well in ways that directly benefit their careers.

Further Research
To better understand the nature of stress among students, it is also important to understand how faculty stress affects the student/faculty relationship. However, only a few published studies focus on the issue of faculty stress. It is very likely that within the student/faculty relationship exists a feedback loop—so that students' and faculty members' stress reactions affect each other. Ultimately, the emotional climate created in the classroom affects teaching, learning, and students' stress reactions. More research

in this area is crucial to improve understanding of stress among students.

With respect to undergraduate students, it would be useful to see the effects better teachers for introductory courses have on reducing stress and on encouraging performance beyond the undergraduate years. One obvious difficulty with this suggestion is that often the best teachers prefer to teach and work with more senior or graduate students.

Research about graduate students could focus more on specific graduate programs. What are the stresses unique to MBA programs, nursing, social work, engineering? Such research is necessary to more accurately understand and be helpful to specific graduate student groups.

Relatively few studies look at stress among law students. Further, most of the information about stress among law students is anecdotal. Many of the actual studies have methodological problems, largely because of their retrospective design, questionable group comparisons, and inability to generalize the results beyond Ivy League schools. More descriptive studies with improved designs across a wider spectrum of law schools will increase the understanding of stress among this student population.

Stress among medical students and residents has clearly been researched more than for other student groups. The benefit of more descriptive studies of this population is probably not as great as a greater focus on intervention strategies. More research is needed to determine how medical schools can most effectively intervene to help their students and residents reduce stress.

Finally, improved teaching ultimately helps to reduce student stress. This belief suggests that faculty development programs should focus not only on improving teaching but also on determining the nature of the relationship between stress among students and the quality of teaching.

REFERENCES

The ERIC Clearinghouse on Higher Education abstracts and indexes the current literature on higher education for the National Institute of Education's monthly bibliographic journal *Resources in Education*. Most of these publications are available through the ERIC Document Reproduction Service (EDRS). For publications cited in this bibliography that are available from EDRS, ordering number and price are included. Readers who wish to order a publication should write to the ERIC Document Reproduction Service, P.O. Box 190, Arlington, Virginia 22210. When ordering, please specify the document number. Documents are available as noted in microfiche (MF) and paper copy (PC). Because prices are subject to change, it is advisable to check the latest issue of *Resources in Education* for current cost based on the number of pages in the publication.

Abramson, Lyn Y.; Garber, J.; and Seligman, M. E. P. 1980. "Learned Helplessness in Humans: An Attributional Analysis." In *Human Helplessness: Theory and Applications,* edited by Judy Garber and M. E. P. Seligman. New York: Academic Press.

Adsett, C. Alex. June 1968. "Psychological Health of Medical Students in Relation to the Medical Education Process." *Journal of Medical Education* 43:728–34.

Altbach, Philip G. December 1970. "Commitment and Powerlessness on the American Campus: The Case of the Graduate Student." *Liberal Education* 56:562–82.

Asken, Michael J., and Raham, David C. May 1983. "Resident Performance and Sleep Deprivation: A Review." *Journal of Medical Education* 58:382–88.

Bargar, Robert R., and Duncan, James K. January-February 1982. "Cultivating Creative Endeavor in Doctoral Research." *Journal of Higher Education* 53:1–36.

Bargar, Robert R., and Mayo-Chamberlin, Jane. July-August 1983. "Advisor and Advisee Issues in Doctoral Education." *Journal of Higher Education* 54:407–32.

Bates, Erica M., and Carroll, Philomena J. November 1975. "Stress in Hospitals: The Married Intern: Vintage 1973." *Medical Journal of Australia* 2:763–65.

Bates, Erica M.; Hinton, Jane; and Wood, Trevor J. September 1973. "Unhappiness and Discontent: A Study of Junior Resident Medical Officers." *Medical Journal of Australia* 2:606–12.

Baum, Andrew; Singer, J. E.; and Baum, C. S. Winter 1981. "Stress and the Environment." *Journal of Social Issues* 37: 4–35.

Becker, H. S.; Geer, B.; Hughes, E. C.; and Strauss, A. L. 1961. *Boys in White: Student Culture in Medical School.* Chicago: University of Chicago Press.

Berdre, Ralph F. 1966. "Student Ambivalence and Behavior." In *The College and the Student,* edited by L. E. Dennis and J. F. Kaufman. Washington, D.C.: American Council on Education.

Berne, Eric. 1964. *Games People Play.* New York: Grove Press.

Blaine, Graham B., Jr., and McArthur, Charles C., eds. 1971. *Emotional Problems of the Student.* 2d ed. New York: Appleton-Century-Crofts.

Bloom, Bernard, ed. 1975. *Psychological Stress in the Campus Community.* New York: Human Sciences Press.

Bojar, S. 1971. "Psychiatric Problems of Medical Students." In *Emotional Problems of the Student,* edited by G. B. Blaine, Jr., and C. C. McArthur. 2d ed. New York: Appleton-Century-Crofts.

Bowers, W. J. 1964. *Student Dishonesty and Its Control in College.* New York: Bureau of Applied Social Research, Columbia University.

Boyle, Blake P., and Coombs, Robert H. October 1971. "Personality Profiles Related to Emotional Stress in the Initial Year of Medical Training." *Journal of Medical Education* 46:882–87.

Breneman, David W. 1975. *Graduate School Adjustment to the "New Depression" in Higher Education.* Washington, D.C.: National Board on Graduate Education. ED 101 643. 105 pp. MF–$1.17; PC–$11.12.

Brent, David A. May 1981. "The Residency as a Developmental Process." *Journal of Medical Education* 56:417–22.

Breo, Dennis. 5 May 1978. "Developing a 'Survival Manual' for Residents' Struggle to Cope with Stress." *American Medical News:* 7–8.

Callan, John P. 1983. *The Physician: A Profession under Stress.* New York: Appleton-Century-Crofts.

Carnegie Commission on Higher Education. 1971. *New Students and New Places.* New York: McGraw-Hill.

Chan, Kwok Bun. January 1977. "Individual Differences in Reactions to Stress and Their Personality and Situational Determinants: Some Implications for Community Mental Health." *Social Science and Medicine* 11:89–103.

Chickering, Arthur W. 1969. *Education and Identity.* San Francisco: Jossey-Bass.

Cleugh, M. F. February 1972. "Stresses of Mature Students." *British Journal of Educational Studies* 20:76–90.

Cobb, Sydney. September-October 1976. "Social Support as a Moderator of Life Stress." *Psychosomatic Medicine* 38:300–14.

Cockerham, William C. 1982. *Medical Sociology.* 2d rev. ed. Englewood Cliffs, N.J.: Prentice-Hall.

Cohen, Sheldon. July 1980. "Aftereffects of Stress on Human Performance and Social Behavior: A Review of Research and Theory." *Psychological Bulletin* 88:82–108.

Cooper, John D. August 1974. "Graduate Medical Education: Whose Responsibility." *Hospitals* 48:47–50.

Cousins, Norman. January 1981. "Internship: Preparation or Hazing?" *Journal of the American Medical Association* 245:377.

Dalrymple, Williard. 1971. "Faculty Counseling and Referral." In *Emotional Problems of the Student,* edited by G. B. Blaine, Jr., and C. C. McArthur. 2d ed. New York: Appleton-Century-Crofts.

DeMille, Barbara. 24 April 1983. "College Student '83: Wary Commitment." *The New York Times Education Spring Survey:* 71.

Dietrick, John E., and Berson, Robert C. 1953. *Medical Schools in the United States.* New York: McGraw-Hill.

Edwards, Marc T., and Zimet, Carl N. August 1976. "Problems and Concerns among Medical Students—1975." *Journal of Medical Education* 51:619–25.

Ellinwood, Steven; Mayerson, N.; and Paul, S. C. 1983. "Law Student Survey Results: An Empirical Method for Assessing Stress in Professional Education Programs: An Assessment of Stress among Law Students at the University of Utah." Mimeographed. Salt Lake City: University of Utah.

Ellis, A. 1962. *Reason and Emotion in Psychotherapy.* New York: Lyle Stuart.

―――. 1970. *The Essence of Rational Psychotherapy: A Comprehensive Approach to Treatment.* New York: Institute for Rational Living.

Ellis, Ving. 1969. "Students Who Seek Psychiatric Help." In *No Time for Youth,* edited by J. Katz. San Francisco: Jossey-Bass.

Erikson, Erik. 1980. *Identity and Life Cycle.* New York: W. W. Norton & Co.

Eron, Leonard D., and Redmount, R. S. 1957. "The Effect of Legal Education on Attitudes." *Journal of Legal Education* 9(4):431–43.

Falk, David. 1975. "Campus Environments, Student Stress, and Campus Planning." In *Psychological Stress in the Campus Community,* edited by B. Bloom. New York: Behavioral Publications.

Farnsworth, Dana L., and Munter, Preston K. 1971. "The Role of the College Psychiatrist." In *Emotional Problems of the Student,* edited by G. B. Blaine, Jr., and C. C. McArthur. 2d ed. New York: Appleton-Century-Crofts.

Feldman, S. D. 1974. *Escape from the Doll's House: Women in Graduate and Professional School Education.* New York: McGraw-Hill.

Finney, Ben C. 1975. "The Peer Program: An Experiment in Humanistic Education." In *Psychological Stress in the Campus Community,* edited by B. Bloom. New York: Behavioral Publications.

Folkman, Susan. 1982. "An Approach to the Measurement of Coping." *Journal of Occupational Behavior* 3(1):95–107.

Frank, Alan. 1966. "Patterns of Student Stress." In *The College and the Student,* edited by L. E. Dennis and J. F. Kaufman. Washington, D.C.: American Council on Education.

Friedman, Richard C.; Bigger, J. Thomas; and Kornfeld, Donald S. July 1971. "The Intern and Sleep Loss." *New England Journal of Medicine* 285:201–3.

Friedman, Richard C.; Kornfeld, Donald S.; and Bigger, J. Thomas. May 1973. "Psychological Problems Associated with Sleep Deprivation in Interns." *Journal of Medical Education* 48:436–41.

Funkenstein, Daniel H. August 1968. "The Learning and Personal Development of Medical Students and Recent Changes in Universities and Medical Schools." *Journal of Medical Education* 43:883–97.

Gaensbauer, Theodore J., and Mizner, George L. February 1980. "Developmental Stresses in Medical Education." *Psychiatry* 43:60–70.

Gellhorn, Alfred. 1979. "It Is Possible to Become Educated While Studying to Become a Doctor." In *Medical Education since 1960,* edited by A. D. Hunt and L. E. Weeks. East Lansing: Michigan State University Foundation.

Giddan, Norman S., and Austin, M. J., eds. 1982. *Peer Counseling and Self-Help Groups on Campus.* Springfield, Ill.: Charles C. Thomas Publisher.

Gilbert, Marvin G. March 1982. "The Impact of Graduate School on the Family: A Systems View." *Journal of College Student Personnel* 23:128–35.

Gilman, Daniel Coit. 1961. "Daniel Coit Gilman Reviews the Accomplishments of the University Era, 1869–1902." In *American Higher Education Documentary History,* edited by R. Hofstadter and W. Smith, vol. 2. Chicago: University of Chicago Press.

Glass, David C., and Singer, J. E. 1972. *Urban Stress: Experiments on Noise and Social Stressors.* New York: Academic Press.

Gottheil, Edward; Thornton, C. C.; Conly, S. S.; and Cornelison, F. S., Jr. April 1969. "Stress, Satisfaction, and Performance: Transition from University to Medical College." *Journal of Medical Education* 44:270–77.

Halleck, Seymour. 1976. "Emotional Problems of the Graduate Student." In *Scholars in the Making,* edited by J. Katz and R. T. Hartnett. Cambridge, Mass.: Ballinger Publishing Co.

Harno, Albert J. 1953. *Legal Education in the United States.* San Francisco: Bancroft Whitney Co.

Hartnett, Rodney T., and Katz, Joseph. 1976. "Past and Present." In *Scholars in the Making,* edited by J. Katz and R. T. Hartnett. Cambridge, Mass.: Ballinger Publishing Co.

Hartshorn, Kay. 1976. "A Day in the Life of a Graduate Student." In *Scholars in the Making,* edited by J. Katz and R. T. Hartnett. Cambridge, Mass.: Ballinger Publishing Co.

Heins, Marilyn, and Fahey, Shirley Nichols. November 1981. "A Comparison of Perceived Stress Levels among Medical and Law Students." Paper presented at the Research in Medical Education Annual Meeting, Washington, D.C.

Heiss, Ann M. 1970. *Challenges to Graduate Schools.* San Francisco: Jossey-Bass.

Hershey, Paul, and Blanchard, Kenneth H. 1972. *Management of Organization Behavior.* Englewood Cliffs, N.J.: Prentice-Hall.

Hirsch, Steven J., and Keniston, Kenneth. February 1970. "Psychosocial Issues in Talented College Dropouts." *Psychiatry* 33:1–20.

Hockey, Robert. 1979. "Stress and the Cognitive Components of Skilled Performance." In *Human Stress and Cognition,* edited by Vernon Hamilton and David M. Warbutin. New York: John Wiley & Sons.

Howell, M. November 1974. "Stop the Treadmill: We Want to Get Off." *The New Physician* 23:27–30.

Huebner, Louis A.; Royer, Jerry A.; and Moore, James. July 1981. "The Assessment and Remediation of Dysfunctional Stress in Medical School." *Journal of Medical Education* 56:547–58.

Hunter, R.C.A.; Lohrenz, J.G.; and Schwartzman, A.E. August 1964. "Nosophobia and Hypochondriasis in Medical Students." *Journal of Nervous and Mental Disease* 139:147–52.

Hunter, R.C.A.; Prince, R.H.; and Schwartzman, A.E. October 1961. "Comments on Emotional Disturbances in a Medical Undergraduate Population." *Canadian Medical Assn. Journal* 85:989–92.

Jacks, Penelope, et al. Spring 1983. "The ABCs of ABDs: A Study of Incomplete Doctorates." *Improving College and University Teaching* 31:74–81.

Janis, Irving L. 1982. "Decision Making under Stress." In *Handbook of Stress: Theoretical and Clinical Aspects,* edited by L. Goldberger and Shlomo Bregnitz. New York: Free Press.

Jencks, Christopher, and Riesman, David. 1969. *The Academic Revolution.* Garden City, N.Y.: Doubleday & Co.

Jenkins, David C. 1979. "Psychosocial Modifiers of Response to Stress." In *Stress and Mental Disorder,* edited by James E. Barrett et al. New York: Raven Press.

Johnson, William R. 1978. *Schooled Lawyers: A Study in Clash of Professional Cultures.* New York: New York University Press.

Kalafat, John, and Schulman, Andi. 1982. "Telephone Crisis Counseling Service." In *Peer Counseling and Self-Help Groups on Campus,* edited by N.S. Giddan and M.J. Austin. Springfield, Ill.: Charles C. Thomas Publisher.

Katz, Joseph. 1975. "Epilogue." In *Psychological Stress in the Campus Community,* edited by B. Bloom. New York: Behavioral Publications.

Katz, Joseph, et al. 1969. *No Time for Youth: Growth and Constraint in College Students.* San Francisco: Jossey-Bass.

Katz, Joseph, and Hartnett, Rodney T., eds. 1976. *Scholars in the Making.* Cambridge, Mass.: Ballinger Publishing Co.

Kerr, Clark. 1963. *The Uses of the University.* New York: Harper & Row.

Kjerulff, Kristen, and Wiggins, N. H. June 1976. "Graduate Student Styles for Coping with Stressful Situations." *Journal of Educational Psychology* 68:247–54.

Knox, Wilma J. November 1970. "Obtaining a Ph.D. in Psychology." *American Psychologist* 25:1026–32.

Kolko, David J. 1980. "Stress Management Techniques for Graduate Students: Cognitive Coping, Problem-Solving and Time Management." Paper presented at the annual meeting of the Southeastern Psychological Association, March, Washington, D.C. ED 192 230. 15 pp. MF–$1.17; PC–$3.74.

Lazarus, Richard S. 1966. *Psychological Stress and the Coping Process.* New York: McGraw-Hill.

Lazarus, Richard S.; Averill J. R.; and Opton, E. M. 1974. "The Psychology of Coping: Issues of Research and Assessment." In *Coping and Adaptation,* edited by G. V. Coelhe, D. A. Hamburg, and J. E. Adams. New York: Basic Books.

Lazarus, Richard S., and Cohen, J. B. 1977. "Environmental Stress." In *Human Behavior and Environment,* edited by I. Altman and J. F. Wohlwill. New York: Plenum Press.

LeFevre, Carol. February 1982. "The Mature Woman as Graduate Student." *School Review* 80:281–98.

Levine, Seymour, and Ursin, Holger, eds. 1981. *Coping and Health.* New York: Plenum Press.

Lief, Harold I.; Young, Kathleen; Sprinell, Vann; Lancaster, Robert R.; and Lief, V.F. July 1960. "A Psychodynamic Study of Medical Students and Their Adaptational Problems: Preliminary Report." *Journal of Medical Education* 35:696–704.

Lockmiller, David. 1969. *Scholars on Parade.* London: The Macmillan Co.

Loewenberg, Peter. November 1969. "Emotional Problems of Graduate Education." *Journal of Higher Education* 40:610–23.

McArthur, Charles C., and Dinklage, Kenneth T. 1971. "The Role of the Psychologist in a College Health Service." In *Emotional Problems of the Student,* edited by G. B. Blaine, Jr., and C. C. McArthur. 2d ed. New York: Appleton-Century-Crofts.

McClelland, David C., et al. 1953. *The Achievement Motive.* New York: Appleton-Century-Crofts.

McKay, Matthew; Davis, M.; and Fanning, P. 1981. *Thoughts and Feelings: The Art of Cognitive Stress Intervention.* Richmond: New Harbinger Publications.

McRoy, Sue, and Fisher, V. L. January 1982. "Marital Adjustment of Graduate Student Couples." *Family Relations* 31:37–41.

Mason, L. John. 1980. *Guide to Stress Reduction.* Culver City, Cal.: Peace Press.

Mayhew, Lewis B. 1970. *Graduate and Professional Education, 1980.* New York: McGraw-Hill.

Mechanic, David. 1978. *Students under Stress: A Study in the Social Psychology of Adaptation.* 2d rev. ed. Madison: University of Wisconsin Press.

Meichenbaum, Donald. 1977. *Cognitive Behavior Modification: An Integrative Approach.* New York: Plenum Press.

Merkel, William T., and Walbroehl, Gordon S. April 1980. "The Annual Third-Year Resident Rampage: A Separation Crisis of Manageable Proportions." *Journal of Medical Education* 55:366–67.

Miller, Paul Van R. 1967. "Personality Differences and Student Survival in Law School." *Journal of Legal Education* 19(1):460–67.

Miller, Roscoe E. November 1981. "The Stresses of Training: A Preceptor's Perceptions." *American Journal of Roentgenology* 137:1088–90.

Miller, Suzanne M. 1980. "Why Having Control Reduces Stress: If I Can Stop the Roller Coaster, I Don't Want to Get Off." In *Human Helplessness: Theory and Application,* edited by J. Garber and M.E.P. Seligman. New York: Academic Press.

Montgomery, L. June. Spring 1972. "Student Anxiety and Graduate Study." *Colorado Journal of Educational Research* 2:24–26.

Moos, Rudolf H. 1974. "Psychological Technique in the Assessment of Adaptive Behavior." In *Coping and Adaptation,* edited by G.V. Coelho, D.A. Hamburg, and J.E. Adams. New York: Basic Books.

Mumford, Emily. May 1983. "Stress in the Medical Career." *Journal of Medical Education* 58:436–37.

Nelson, Robert L. 1971. "Special Problems of Graduate Students in the School of Arts and Sciences." In *Emotional Problems of the Student,* edited by G.B. Blaine, Jr., and C.C. McArthur. 2d ed. New York: Appleton-Century-Crofts.

Nisbet, Robert. Autumn 1979. "The Octopus Revisited." *Social Research* 46:488–516.

Norman, Mary. 1970. "Troubled Students: In Departments, in Fields, and in Professional Associations of Higher Education." Paper presented at the 25th National Conference on Higher Education, 3 March, Chicago, Illinois. ED 038 084. 14 pp. MF–$1.17; PC–$3.74.

Patton, Michael J. 1968. "The Student, the Situation, and Performance during the First Year of Law School." *Journal of Legal Education* 21(1):10–51.

Payne, Roy; Todd, D.J.; and Burke, R. J. 1982. "Whither Stress Research? An Agenda for the 1980s." *Journal of Occupational Behaviour* 3(1):131–45.

Pfeiffer, Roxane Javid. February 1983. "Early-Adult Development in the Medical Student." *Mayo Clinic Proceedings* 58:127–34.

Pipkin, Ronald M. Fall 1976. "Legal Education: The Consumers' Perspective." *American Bar Foundation Research Journal* 4:1161–92.

Rosenberg, Pearl P. March 1971. "Students' Perceptions and Concerns during Their First Year in Medical School." *Journal of Medical Education* 46:211–18.

Rudolph, Frederick. 1962. *The American College and University.* New York: Vintage Books.

Sanford, Mark. 1976. *Making It in Graduate School.* Berkeley: Montaigne.

Sanford, Nevitt, ed. 1967a. *The American College.* New York: John Wiley & Sons.

———. 1967b. *Where Colleges Fail.* San Francisco: Jossey-Bass.

Saslow, George. January 1956. "Symposium on the Medical Student: Psychiatric Problems of Medical Students." *Journal of Medical Education* 31:27–33.

Schoonmaker, Alan N. 1971. *A Students' Survival Manual or How to Get an Education Despite It All.* New York: Harper & · Row.

Schwarz, Arthur H.; Schwartzburg, M.; Lieb, I.; and Slaby, A.E. July 1978. "Medical School and the Process of Disillusionment." *Medical Education* 12:182–85.

Seigle, Richard D.; Schuckit, Marc A.; and Plumb, Diane. July 1983. "Availability of Personal Counseling in Medical Schools." *Journal of Medical Education* 58:542–46.

Seligman, Martin E.P. 1975. *Helplessness: On Depression, Development, and Death.* San Francisco: W. H. Freeman.

Selye, Hans. July 1936. "A Syndrome Produced by Diverse Nocuous Agents." *Nature* 138:32.

———. June 1975. "Confusion and Controversy in the Stress Field." *Journal of Human Stress* 1:37–44.

———. 1976. *The Stress of Life.* New York: McGraw-Hill.

———, ed. 1980. *Selye's Guide to Stress Research.* New York: Van Nostrand Reinhold Co.

———. 1982. "History and Present Status of the Stress Concept." In *Handbook of Stress: Theoretical and Clinical Aspects,* edited by L. Goldberger and S. Breznitz. New York: Free Press.

Shapiro, E., and Driscoll, S. 1979. "Effects of Time-Intensive Nature of Graduate Medical Education." In *Becoming a Physician,* edited by E. Shapiro and L. Lowenstein. Cambridge, Mass.: Ballinger Publishing Co.

Sherburne, Philip. 1966. "Before the Doctor Comes: Conditions of Stress on the Campus." In *The College and the Student,* edited by L.E. Dennis and J.F. Kaufman. Washington, D.C.: American Council on Education.

Siegel, Benjamin, and Donnelly, Julie C. November 1978. "Enriching Personal and Professional Development: The Experience of a Support Group for Interns." *Journal of Medical Education* 53:908–14.

Sierles, Frederick; Hendrick, Ingrid; and Circle, Sybil. February 1980. "Cheating in Medical School." *Journal of Medical Education* 55:124–25.

Silver, Lawrence. 1968. "Anxiety and the First Semester of Law School." *Wisconsin Law Review* 4(4):1201–18.

Smith, G. Kerry, ed. 1968. *Stress and Campus Response*. San Francisco: Jossey-Bass.

———, ed. 1970. *The Troubled Campus*. San Francisco: Jossey-Bass.

Smith, Virginia, and Bernstein, Alison R. 1979. *The Impersonal Campus*. San Francisco: Jossey-Bass.

Snyder, Berson R. 1966. "The Invisible Curriculum." In *The College and the Student,* edited by L.E. Dennis and J.F. Kaufman. Washington, D.C.: American Council on Education.

Solomon, Lewis C. 1976. *Male and Female Graduate Students: The Question of Equality*. New York: Praeger.

Stevens, Robert. April 1973. "Law School and Law Students." *Virginia Law Review* 59:551–707.

Stevens, Rosemary. 1971. *American Medicine and the Public Interest*. New Haven: Yale University Press.

Stone, Alan A. December 1971. "Legal Education on the Couch." *Harvard Law Review* 85:392–441.

Suszek, Robert F. 1972. *The Best Laid Plans*. San Francisco: Jossey-Bass.

Taylor, James B. 1975. "Law School Stress and the Deformation Professionelle." *Journal of Legal Education* 27(3):251–67.

Tokarz, J.P.; Bremer, W.; and Peters, K. 1979. *Beyond Survival*. Chicago: American Medical Association.

Turow, Scott. 1977. *One L*. New York: Penguin Books.

Vaillant, George E. 1977. *Adaptation to Life*. Boston: Little Brown & Co.

Valdez, Ramiro. Spring 1982. "First Year Doctoral Students and Stress." *College Student Journal* 16:30–37.

Valko, Robert J., and Clayton, Paul J. January 1975. "Depression in the Internship." *Diseases of the Nervous System* 36:26–29.

Walker, Marion, and Beach, Mark. 1976. *Making It in College*. New York: Mason/Charter Publishers.

Watson, Andrew S. Winter 1968. "The Quest for Professional Competence: Psychological Aspects of Legal Education." *Cincinnati Law Review* 37:93–166.

Webster, Thomas G., and Robinowitz, Carol B. January 1979. "Becoming a Physician: Long-Term Student Group." *General Hospital Psychiatry* 1:53–61.

Weinstein, Harvey. May 1983. "A Committee on Well-Being of Medical Students and House Staff." *Journal of Medical Education* 58:373–81.

White, Robert W. 1974. "Strategies of Adaptation: An Attempt at Systematic Description." In *Coping and Adaptation,* edited by G.V. Coelho, D.A. Hamburg, and J.E. Adams. New York: Basic Books.

Wilkinson, R.; Tyler P.; and Varey, C. October 1975. "Duty Hours of Young Hospital Doctors: Effects on the Quality of Their Work." *Journal of Occupational Psychology* 48:219–29.

Willingham, Warren W. January 1974. "Predicting Success in Graduate Education." *Science* 183:273–78.

Woods, Sharon M.; Natterson, Joseph; and Silverson, Jerome. August 1966. "Medical Students' Disease: Hypochondriasis in Medical Education." *Journal of Medical Education* 41:785–90.

Yerkes, Robert M., and Dodson, J.D. November 1908. "The Relation of Strength of Stimulus to Rapidity of Habit Formation." *Journal of Comparative and Neurological Psychology* 18:459–82.

ASHE-ERIC HIGHER EDUCATION RESEARCH REPORTS

Starting in 1983, the Association for the Study of Higher Education assumed cosponsorship of the Higher Education Research Reports with the ERIC Clearinghouse on Higher Education. For the previous 11 years, ERIC and the American Association for Higher Education prepared and published the reports.

Each report is the definitive analysis of a tough higher education problem, based on a thorough research of pertinent literature and institutional experiences. Report topics, identified by a national survey, are written by noted practitioners and scholars with prepublication manuscript reviews by experts.

Ten monographs in the ASHE-ERIC Higher Education Research Report series are published each year, available individually or by subscription. Subscription to 10 issues is $55 regular; $40 for members of AERA, AAHE, and AIR; $35 for members of ASHE. (Add $7.50 outside U.S.)

Prices for single copies, including 4th class postage and handling, are $7.50 regular and $6.00 for members of AERA, AAHE, AIR, and ASHE. If faster 1st class postage is desired for U.S. and Canadian orders, for each publication ordered add $.75; for overseas, add $4.50. For VISA and MasterCard payments, give card number, expiration date, and signature. Orders under $25 must be prepaid. Bulk discounts are available on orders of 10 or more of a single title. Order from the Publications Department, Association for the Study of Higher Education, One Dupont Circle, Suite 630, Washington, D.C. 20036, (202) 296-2597. Write for a complete list of Higher Education Research Reports and other ASHE and ERIC publications.

1981 Higher Education Research Reports

1. Minority Access to Higher Education
   Jean L. Preer

2. Institutional Advancement Strategies in Hard Times
   Michael D. Richards and Gerald Sherratt

3. Functional Literacy in the College Setting
   Richard C. Richardson, Jr., Kathryn J. Martens, and Elizabeth C. Fisk

4. Indices of Quality in the Undergraduate Experience
   George D. Kuh

5. Marketing in Higher Education
   Stanley M. Grabowski

6. Computer Literacy in Higher Education
   Francis E. Masat

7. Financial Analysis for Academic Units
   Donald L. Walters

8. Assessing the Impact of Faculty Collective Bargaining
   J. Victor Baldridge, Frank R. Kemerer, and Associates

9. Strategic Planning, Management, and Decision Making
   Robert G. Cope

10. Organizational Communication in Higher Education
    Robert D. Gratz and Philip J. Salem

1982 Higher Education Research Reports

1. Rating College Teaching: Criterion Studies of Student
   Evaluation-of-Instruction Instruments
   Sidney E. Benton

2. Faculty Evaluation: The Use of Explicit Criteria for
   Promotion, Retention, and Tenure
   Neal Whitman and Elaine Weiss

3. The Enrollment Crisis: Factors, Actors, and Impacts
   *J. Victor Baldridge, Frank R. Kemerer, and Kenneth C.
   Green*

4. Improving Instruction: Issues and Alternatives for Higher
   Education
   Charles C. Cole, Jr.

5. Planning for Program Discontinuance: From Default to
   Design
   Gerlinda S. Melchiori

6. State Planning, Budgeting, and Accountability: Approaches
   for Higher Education
   Carol E. Floyd

7. The Process of Change in Higher Education Institutions
   Robert C. Nordvall

8. Information Systems and Technological Decisions: A Guide
   for Non-Technical Administrators
   Robert L. Bailey

9. Government Support for Minority Participation in Higher
   Education
   Kenneth C. Green

10. The Department Chair: Professional Development and Role
    Conflict
    David B. Booth

1983 Higher Education Research Reports

1. The Path to Excellence: Quality Assurance in Higher
   Education
   *Laurence R. Marcus, Anita O. Leone, and Edward D.
   Goldberg*

2. Faculty Recruitment, Retention, and Fair Employment: Obligations and Opportunities
   John S. Waggaman

3. Meeting the Challenges: Developing Faculty Careers
   Michael C. T. Brookes and Katherine L. German

4. Raising Academic Standards: A Guide to Learning Improvement
   Ruth Talbott Keimig

5. Serving Learners at a Distance: A Guide to Program Practices
   Charles E. Feasley

6. Competence, Admissions, and Articulation: Returning to the Basics in Higher Education
   Jean L. Preer

7. Public Service in Higher Education: Practices and Priorities
   Patricia H. Crosson

8. Academic Employment and Retrenchment: Judicial Review and Administrative Action
   Robert M. Hendrickson and Barbara A. Lee

9. Burnout: The New Academic Disease
   Winifred Albizu Meléndez and Rafael M. de Guzmán

10. Academic Workplace: New Demands, Heightened Tensions
    Ann E. Austin and Zelda F. Gamson

1984 Higher Education Research Reports

1. Adult Learning: State Policies and Institutional Practices
   K. Patricia Cross and Anne-Marie McCartan

2. Student Stress: Effects and Solutions
   Neal A. Whitman, David C. Spendlove, and Claire H. Clark

DATE DUE

MAY 1 3 2004		
MAY 1 1 2004		

GAYLORD   PRINTED IN U.S.A